HEAL YOUR MIND

TO HEAL YOUR BODY

INDRONEIL MUKERJEE
ASSISTED BY APOORVA JAIN

Chennai • Bangalore

CLEVER FOX PUBLISHING
Chennai, India

Published by CLEVER FOX PUBLISHING 2025
Copyright © Indroneil Mukerjee 2025

All Rights Reserved.
ISBN: 978-93-67074-15-2

No part of this publication may be reproduced or transmitted, in any form or by any mechanical, photographic, or electronic process, or in the form of a phonographic recording, nor may it be stored in a retrieval system or otherwise be copied for public or private use other than for "fair use" as brief quotations embodied in articles and reviews, without prior written permission of the publisher.

This book is sold subject to the condition that it shall not by way of trade or otherwise, be sold, re-sold or otherwise circulated in any form of binding, cover or title other than in which it is published.

Persistent efforts are made and utmost care has been taken while preparing this book. Inspite of this, some mistakes or omissions might have crept into it. The author, publisher, or anybody in the line of sale of this book shall not be liable for any action - civil, criminal or otherwise - for any damage or inconvenience caused as a result of misinterpretation or misapplication of the law or due to any inadvertent mistake or omission. Sale of this book is subject to the foregoing conditions.

The views and opinions expressed in this book are the author's own and the facts are as reported by him, and the publishers are not in any way liable for the same.

The author of this book does not dispense medical advice or prescribe the use of any technique as a form of treatment for physical, emotional, or medical problems without the advice of a physician, either directly or indirectly. The intent of the author is only to offer information of a general nature to help readers in quest for emotional and spiritual well-being. In the event readers use any of the information in this book for themselves, which is their constitutional right, the author and the publisher assumes no responsibility for readers' actions.

Foreword 1

It gives me a great pleasure and I consider it indeed as an honour to be invited by Indroneil to write a foreword for the title "Heal your Mind to Heal your Body" which he is about to publish.

Before I write anything about the book which has been authored by him so painstakingly, let me begin by saying that it has been an absolute privilege to have known Indroneil as a person, as a human being. A human being who is so extremely talented, gifted, passionate and full with wisdom across different walks of life – be it his mastery over multiple languages, his music, his love for fine food, his laughter, and the fullness that he radiates to everyone who meets him.

An amazing Coach and Teacher. A voice who is worth its weight in gold. That's who he really is.

I studied Bach Flower Therapies and their application through him – he has been my personal therapist to begin with and later my personal mentor in this field.

Whatever little I have come to know about the transformational Bach Flower medicine and their effects on human body and mind, through the little practice I have run; the credit entirely and unequivocally goes to Indroneil.

It is only due to his constant push, nudge. Motivation and encouragement that I am a practicing Bach flower therapist today – the phase I am enjoying beyond description.

Bach flower therapies actually heal. But behind the administration of these therapies there is Healer. A healer who practices this science through words, concepts, affection, therapy, and emotions – everything comes together to deliver the crescendo effect of having gotten calmed and repaired from deep within for his patients and students - Indroneil is a tall healer. In the category of greats.

His dedication, passion and commitment to take Bach Flower Medicine to as many as possible is not only commendable but almost spiritual.

The Book – "Heal your Mind to Heal your Body" was in the works for a long time. This is his creation where he has not only documented the years of wisdom but has practically poured out his heart for the benefit of our society. This is an amazing read and must have in the book shelves.

Good Luck, Dada! My tons of best wishes to you always. May you be blessed with the best of the health as you look ahead.

I am grateful to the universe to have found you, known you, experienced you and worked with you.

You changed me forever.

More power to you.

KEDAR APSHANKAR
Ex- CEO, President and COO with Aditya Birla Group.

FOREWORD 2

Indroneil Mukerjee, one of the most experienced Bach flower therapists in India, has succeeded in showing a comprehensible path in the book "Heal your Mind to heal your Body" that meets the WHO's claim of complete physical, mental and social well-being. In his holistic approach, he describes in simple and easy-to-understand terms how illness arises from negative thoughts and negative emotions and is never an isolated physical process. The first chapter is very well done and I recommend it to be read. The explanation of how illness manifests itself through the psyche is brilliant. I have never read any other book that explains this so perfectly and, above all, so easily understandable. Our own emotions not only trigger the physical afflictions we complain about, they also influence the course of the illness and shape the way in which we block our healing and thereby harm ourselves. Using clear examples, this disease-causing process becomes understandable and shows the need to treat the actual cause of the illness - negative emotions - and not just their physical consequences using Bach Flower essences.

The description of the 38 Bach Flowers is extraordinary. Indroneil not only describes the negative emotions according to which the individual flowers are prescribed, but also describes the process of transformation that is triggered by the flowers and the resulting positive aspects for the life of the individual. He is not only concerned with eliminating the negative emotions that are responsible for the physical afflictions complained of, but with transforming the personality towards a life in harmony with oneself. Ideally, this means being as free from suffering as possible and using one's full potential. For Indroneil, the Bach Flowers trigger a spiritual process that leads us to our true self.

The subsequent chapters of healing physical ailments with Bach Flower essences offers valuable tips for self-treatment. Deciphering the language of the organs makes it easier for the individual to find the flowers that are suitable for him. In this way, the book is a valuable guide and a must have in one bookshelf to achieving a life in harmony with ourselves, our environment and the cosmos.

DIETMAR KRÄMER

Dietmar Krämer, a licensed naturopath in his native Germany, has been active as a practitioner and teacher of holistic health care since 1983. He is also the author of New Bach Flower Therapies.

I dedicate this offering to all those who have enabled me to bring to surface the knowing that always existed infinitely in the Universe and consolidate it as practice wisdom and knowledge, for the benefit of those on their healing journey.

To my clients, students, mentors and to the Divine Intelligence for channelling through me that which I need to accompany others in their healing journeys.

INDRONEIL

ALCHEMIST, TRANSFORMATIVE HEALING

Indroneil is an internationally acclaimed Bach Flower Practitioner. His specialty is transformative healing with Bach Flower Essences - he enables or causes transformation in the lives of individuals with Bach Flower.

Pursuing his passion or purpose to facilitate transformation in human lives for more than two decades, he has touched around 20,000 lives with and without Bach Flower Essence.

Indroneil is gifted with a keen diagnostic eye and the ability to diagnose illness by listening and sensing the client in a very short time. Besides having researched Bach Flower essences and their transformative effect for over a decade, he has a rich and deep background in applied behavioural science for more than 15 years, and is a Certified Gestalt Psychotherapist and a Transformational Coach. This gives him a solid edge in understanding the nuances of being human and leads him to the root cause of the illness quickly. Indroneil is accredited with several international holistic healing associations. He has been prolifically featured and quoted in the media.

It is to Indroneil's credit that he made transformative healing with Bach Flower Essence a scientific discipline. It is no longer a mystical or ad hoc approach, which has been more popular thus far, which had not allowed the practice to be embraced professionally as much as it should have, by now. Thanks to his effort and intent, the practice of healing with Bach Flower essences has evolved to cause complete transformation in the clients and is rechristened as Floral Alchemy™.

Indroneil is a very powerful educator of people who aspire to practice using Bach Flower, and he runs regular certification classes and coaching sessions.

We are all born to love.

If ever there is an aberration in the others' behaviour, know that there is some difficulty, something is coming in the way.

Coming from this knowing, this belief, it not only helps you to see the block but also helps the other to heal and become whole.

With love!

- Indroneil

Chapter 1
What causes physical ailments?

It is believed that smoking causes cancer, alcohol addiction causes liver damage and over eating causes obesity and other lifestyle diseases.

Is it universally true?

If this is true, what about those who do not contract these ailments despite
overindulging? And what about those who do not indulge in any of these and yet get ill,which sometimes gets fatal too?

KK Menon, a famous Indian singer, tragically passed away at the age of 53 from a heart attack. The CEO of Pepper Fry India also lost his life to cardiac arrest at 51. Comedian Raju Shrivastav died at 58 due to complications following a heart attack. Similarly, Rudratej Singh, Group President and CEO of BMW India, suffered a fatal cardiac arrest at the young age of 46 while working out on a treadmill at home. It is believed that they all led a reasonably healthy lifestyle. How then do we explain this mid-forty – mid -fifty mysterious fatal chasm that celebs tend to fall into? What could be the root causes of such physical ailments?

This isn't just an issue in India. The World Health Organization (WHO) reported in 2021 that globally, cardiovascular diseases (CVDs) were responsible for about 17.9 million deaths in 2019, making up 32% of all deaths worldwide. What's even more striking is that 85% of these deaths were due to heart attacks and strokes. This number is increasing every year.

While it's true that habits such as smoking or alcoholism significantly increase the risk of contracting one or more life-threatening ailment, not every smoker will develop cancer nor heavy drinkers, liver damage. You've probably heard stories of people who seemed to do everything right: eating healthy, being kind, taking care of themselves, yet losing their lives to fatal illnesses. A well-to-do farmer, living in a village, following a natural lifestyle, a non-smoker and teetotaler, lost his life to cirrhosis of liver. It's surprising and sad when this happens because it challenges the belief that a healthy lifestyle guarantees protection from disease.

Is it genetics?

Dr. Bruce Lipton, the father of epigenetics, suggests that our genes don't automatically determine whether we'll get a disease. Instead, he suggests that things like our environment, how we perceive and react to it, can actually influence how our genes behave. While we might have genes linked to certain illnesses, it's the signals from our surroundings and our mindset that can "turn on" or "turn off" these genes. So, it's not just about genetics. It's about how we live and think that really matters.

What then could be root causes of such ailments, healing which will not only heal the diseases but also prevent them from happening? Sparing us from short term 'fixes' (often toxic) or trapped in a lifetime of prescriptions without any permanent cure?

The root causes of most if not all physical ailments are our emotional landscapes at the bottom of which are our limiting beliefs and conditioning.

Dr. Bruce Lipton, known for his work The Biology of Belief, has highlighted how emotions directly impact cellular health through his research in epigenetics. Similarly, Dr. Edward Bach, who developed Bach Flower remedies, emphasised the importance of emotional and

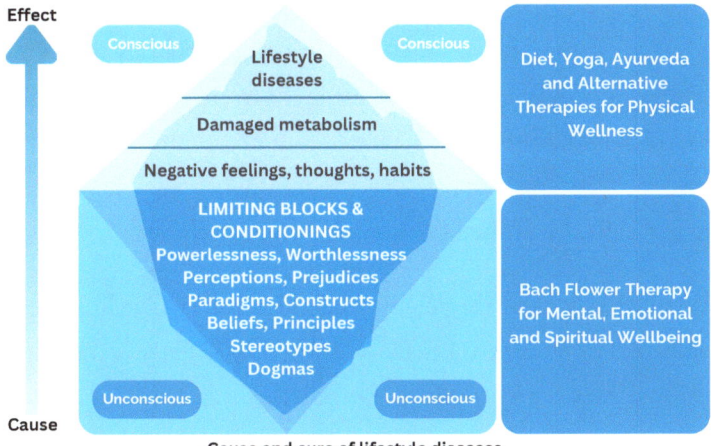

Cause and cure of lifestyle diseases

spiritual well-being in maintaining overall health. Dr. Edward Bach (1886-1936) was a British physician, homoeopath, and bacteriologist. In his work "Heal Thyself," he explains disease thus - **"Disease is the result of conflict between soul and mind and will never be eradicated except by spiritual and mental effort."**

He believed behind all disease lies feelings of fear, anxiety, greed, and worry. When we heal them, we heal the disease from which we suffer. As described by Dr Bach, "The mind, being the most delicate and sensitive part of the body, shows the onset and the course of disease much more definitely than the body, so that the outlook of the mind is chosen as the guide as to which remedy or remedies are necessary" (Edward Bach, The Twelve Healers, 1933).

Even impaired metabolism, which is commonly believed to be the culprit causing lifestyle diseases is not a cause in itself. It's the effect of the beliefs and blocks working silently in the labyrinths of the unconscious, guiding our thoughts, emotions, actions, behaviors and even habits. For example, the emotional cause of heart attack could be squeezing all the joy out of the heart in favour of money or position. All other factors are mere pre-dispositions. They may be considered as causes etiologically – the cause that is not within the individual – which cause dysfunctions within, and that which can only be fixed by fixing the external conditions. For example, diet, exercise, medicines and other correctional means. This way it cannot be healed. Teleologically – the causes, that are within the individual and can therefore be completely healed – are what cause physical ailments.

A powerful example of the teleological approach to healing can be seen in Louise Hay's journey. Louise Hay (1926–2017) was an author and motivational speaker known for her book "You Can Heal Your Life." After being diagnosed with what was considered an incurable cancer, she embraced positive thinking, affirmations, and emotional healing, with the ultimate goal of restoring her overall well-being. Her focus was not just on treating the disease, but on understanding why it manifested and working towards a state of inner harmony and health.

Another discovery called the German New Medicine (GNM) was made by Dr. Ryke Geerd Hamer, a German doctor, in 1981. He began developing GNM after he faced a serious illness following the tragic death of his son. He started exploring how emotional trauma might be connected to physical diseases. He proposed that certain diseases, especially cancer, are triggered by specific emotional shocks or conflicts, which he called "conflict shocks" or "biological conflicts."

Dr. Joe Dispenza is a neuroscientist, author, and speaker who focuses on the power of the mind in healing and personal transformation. In 1986, after a biking accident left him with a severe spinal fracture, he was advised to undergo surgery. Instead, Dr. Dispenza chose to heal himself through meditation and mental focus. By visualizing his spine healing daily, he made a full recovery in a few months without surgery. His experience became the foundation for his teachings on the mind-body connection and self-healing.

A CASE STUDY

Here is a case study from our own practice of Transformative Healing using Bach Flower Essences, wherein you will see how an individual got completely healed from diabetes after her emotions and the underlying blocks got healed.

A couple of years ago, this lady in her mid-fifties, approached me to get healed of her diabetes.

She had earlier enrolled in a diabetes reversal program for six months. She was put under a strict regime of diet and exercise, which she doggedly had to follow, with much dislike and stress. Her, sugar level, nevertheless gradually dropped till it came to normal and she was weaned off her diabetic diet to resume normal but balanced diet. She reportedly followed this for another six months till she realized that bodily symptoms of symptoms of diabetes, like exhaustion, excessive thirst and unusual hunger pangs started creeping in. Her random sugar levels had gone beyond 300 mg/dl and HbA1C a spiraling 13. Her diabetologist immediately put her back on high levels of insulin. That's when she came to us.

I took a two-pronged approach – health coaching which comprised of diet and lifestyle consultation and healing her negative emotions with Bach Flower essences, simultaneously.

Emotionally, she was stubborn, hyper critical, bitter and blaming. Initially she resisted following the guidance of the health coach. She vehemently refused to follow the diabetic diet, which caused further stress. With Bach Flower Essences gently healing her negative emotions and reactionary and rebelling behaviours, she gradually not only started following the advice of the health coach but started enjoying the diet. She was a Yoga enthusiast and got back to diligently practicing it for an hour every day. Within six months here sugar levels came to normal and she was taken off insulin to be put on a maintenance dose of oral anti-diabetic medication. We kept observing her closely for the next six months while she was gradually reintroduced to a balanced diet. Her sugar levels remained normal. What was most heartening was to see her emotionally and behaviourally transformed. She had become more tolerant, suppliant, and forgiving. Instead of donning a victim identity all the time, she got back to her old friends and began enjoying life. At the end of six months, just before completing the program with us, she was taken off medication. Instead, she was put on dietary and other supplements that helped her to maintain her sugar levels at normal.

It matters not what situation you are in.
What matters is your response to the situation.

- Indroneil

Chapter 2
Body mimics the Mind

"Butterflies in the stomach"

"Hair standing on end"

"Goosebumps all over"

"Heart skipped a beat"

"A shiver down my spine"

You've probably heard these idioms countless times. But have you ever thought of why we use them?

Our inner reality reflects in our outward expressions. Our body's reactions are powerful indicators of what we're feeling inside.

The body doesn't just follow the mind; it actively responds to our thoughts and emotions, often without us realizing. When we feel an emotion, the brain releases neurotransmitters, chemical signals that travel throughout the body. These signals impact how we think and how our body reacts to different situations.

For example, if you are stressed, your brain emits hormones such as adrenaline and cortisol, which have physical responses like fast breathing, increased heart rate, and muscle tension. On the other hand, feelings of happiness release endorphins and serotonin, causing relaxed muscles and a sense of well-being.

Mind-Body Connection
Have you ever noticed how your body reacts when you are anxious

or after you hear bad news? Before an important event, you may feel the increase in your heart rate, your stomach might feel jittery, and you might feel uneasy. And when you hear good news, your body feels lighter, like you're almost floating with happiness.

You know, you've gone through this before, even if you weren't aware of it. If you haven't, you can close your eyes and think of something that bothers you, something that really gets to you. Take a moment, really concentrate on it, and note where in your body you're feeling it. Now, let's do the opposite, think about something that brings you happiness. Focus on that thought for a minute. Did you feel that switch? How our bodies have such distinct reactions to positive and negative thoughts and emotions is truly amazing.

The Body mimics the Mind, always.

The Impact of Mental States on Physical Health

Emotions constantly influence our bodies, whether we're aware of it or not. Even small feelings, like frustration or excitement, leave a physical impact. They don't just stay in the mind; they ripple through the body, either building us up or wearing us down over time. Every emotion shapes our physical state, creating tension or relaxation, energy or fatigue.

These emotions also shape how we behave and see the world. When stress, anxiety, or overwhelm become constant, it becomes harder to stay positive or open-minded. You might snap at others, lose patience easily, or shy away from new opportunities because everything feels too overwhelming.

Imagine being caught in a never-ending loop of negative emotions, day in and day out. Think about how much that would wear you down and affect your body over time. Eventually, all that buildup of negative emotions starts to show up as physical ailments. Your body begins to manifest what's been going on inside for so long. For example, people who are sensitive to harsh sounds often suffer from tinnitus. Those who are stiff and stubborn, always wanting things their way, may develop a stiff neck. People who feel overwhelmed or overburdened tend to complain about shoulder pain. And those who resist changes in plans or have a hard time adapting to new ideas might experience problems with their elbows.

Irritable Bowel Syndrome
Chronic diseases, especially of gastrointestinal origin, can be completely healed without any medication if and when their psychological (mental, emotional, and behavioural) causes are healed. For this, it is absolutely necessary to heal the underlying unconscious conditioning (limiting blocks and beliefs) that give rise to negative emotions and behaviours.

In order to understand this phenomenon, let's take the case of IBS – Irritable Bowel Syndrome. IBS is a condition that affects the digestive system and leads to irregular bowel movements. It is classified as a functional disorder, meaning there is no clinical issue with the digestive system.

The mind and the gut are intertwined in what scientists call the gut-brain axis, a 2-way signalling system between the brain and the gut. This links anxiety and IBS too. In the gut-brain axis, our thoughts, feelings, and environment lead to a release of chemicals that affect different processes in our bodies. With IBS and anxiety, the theory is that when one feels anxious, the body releases stress-related chemicals to the gut that can make it more sensitive and inflamed, which ultimately leads to abdominal pain, a change in your gut bacteria, and abnormal bowel movements.

In the other direction, a poorly functioning gut has been linked to mental health problems. This is because the brain depends on chemicals and hormones that are made by the bacteria in the gut. In fact, over 90% of serotonin is made in the gut! Serotonin is an important chemical that controls mood and helps control anxiety levels. Mental health problems can occur when there is too much or too little of it, causing a vicious circle. An intervention that can break this vicious circle by addressing the deep-seated fears and related anxiety, for example, is that which can permanently reverse such a condition.

Physical Ailment	Probable Emotional Cause
Headaches	Invalidating the self. Self-criticism. Fear.
Neck (Cervical Spine):	Represents flexibility. The ability to see what's back there. Refusing to see other sides of a question. Stubbornness, inflexibility. Unbending stubbornness.
Shoulder	Represents our ability to carry out experiences in life joyously. We make life a burden by are attitude. Carrying the burdens of life. Helpless and hopeless.
Heart	**Heart**: Represents the center of love and security. **Heart Attack**: Squeezing all the joy out of the heart in favoUr of money or position. Feeling alone and scared. "I'm not good enough. I don't do enough. I'll never make it." **Heart Problems**: Long standing emotional problems. Lack of joy. Hardening of the heart. Belief in strain and stress.
Stomach	Holds nourishment. Digests ideas. Dread. Fear of the new. Inability to assimilate the new.

Physical Ailment	Probable Emotional Cause
Hip	Carries the body in perfect balance. Major thrust inmoving forward. Fear of going forward in major decisions. Nothing to move forward to.
Elbow	Represents changing directions and accepting newexperiences.
Wrist	Represents movement and ease.
Knee	Represents pride and ego. Stubborn ego and pride. Inability to bend. Fear. Inflexibility. Won't give in.
Ankle(s)	Inflexibility and guilt. Ankles represent the ability to receive pleasure.
Skin	Protects our individuality. Anxiety, fear. Old, buried things. "I am being threatened."
Source: Louise Hay, Heal Your Body	

THE PAIN SCALE

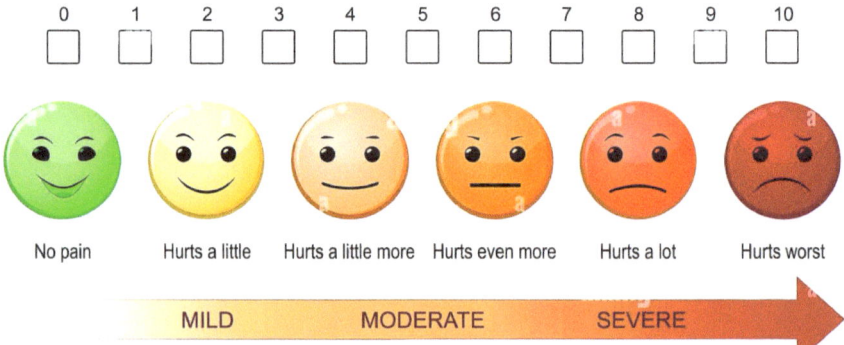

How Physical Actions Shape Our Mental State

It's interesting that body language and emotion influence each other. Research shows that the way we hold ourselves can actually change how we feel. This is called "embodied cognition" or "body feedback." For instance, smiling—even if we're not happy—can make us feel better. Similarly, standing in a "power pose," like standing tall with arms outstretched, can boost confidence and reduce stress.

Our feelings affect how we move, but taking care of our bodies can also change how we feel. Activities like exercise, dancing, getting enough sleep, and being in sunlight can make us feel better. If we don't move enough, we might feel tired or sad. So, our bodies don't just copy our minds; they also help shape our feelings.

In India, for example, the practice of mudras has long been a way to connect mental and physical well-being. People have been using them for thousands of years to feel more centered and connected.

When we practice **yoga, meditation,** and **pranayama** (breathing exercises) it not only relaxes and calms the mind but also affects the body.

Have you ever heard of mudras? Mudra is a Sanskrit word that simply means "gesture." It is a specific hand gesture. Something as simple as touching your fingers in certain ways can have a real impact on both your body and mind. There are many mudras which can be practiced. Stating few common ones below

Gyan Mudra, where you touch your thumb and index finger together. It's great for calming the mind and boosting concentration. By doing this, you're not just making a hand gesture – you're actually helping your mind and body work together to feel more at peace.

When feeling emotionally exhausted, the **Prana Mudra**, made by touching the little and ring fingers to the thumb, is said to revitalize the body and enhance inner strength.

Another useful mudra is **Apana Mudra**, where the middle and ring fingers meet the thumb. This is thought to help release pent-up emotions like anger and frustration.

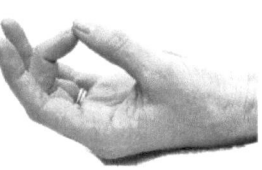

Shuni Mudra, with the middle finger touching the thumb, is often used to cultivate patience and emotional balance, helping with feelings of restlessness or impulsiveness.

The **Anjali Mudra**, where palms are pressed together in front of the chest, is a familiar gesture that promotes a sense of calm, gratitude, and connection. It's often used to center the emotions during meditation or prayer.

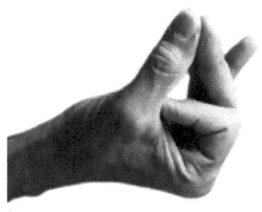

Hridaya Mudra, formed by placing the index finger at the base of the thumb and bringing the middle and the ring fingers to touch the thumb, is known for releasing emotional stress and easing feelings of sadness or heaviness.

Chinmaya Mudra is formed by touching the tips of your thumb and the index finger to form a circle, while the other three fingers curl into your palm. Place your hands on your knees and face the palms upward. It's believed that this mudra helps calm the mind, deepen your breathing, and improve focus.

Merudanda Mudra. To do this mudra, make a loose fist and extend your thumb upward. Rest your hands on your thighs and face the palms upwards. It helps to align the spine and encourage a sense of balance and calmness. This mudra is thought to support better breathing and energy flow along the spine.

These mudras are simple but effective practices that can help balance emotions and promote a harmonious connection between the mind and body.

The body and mind are inseparable, like two sides of the same coin, constantly interacting with each other. It's an ongoing conversation between the two. By carefully observing ourselves, we can often link a physical ailment to its possible emotional cause.

*Truth is only that which you experience
Rest is heresay.*

— *Indroneil*

Chapter 3
Language of Organs

Are you carrying emotional baggage?

Every organ in our body is not just a physical structure; it's deeply connected to our emotions. When we feel something whether it's fear, joy, or anxiety our nervous system sends signals throughout the body. The more we feel a certain way, the more our cells remember that feeling. Over time, this emotional memory starts to shape how we physically respond to life. When an emotion becomes too strong, it can affect how well that organ works.

The link between organs and emotions has been understood since ancient times, like in the Far Eastern school of thoughts of Traditional Chinese Medicine (TCM). TCM identifies five main emotions— anger, fear, grief, worry, grief, and joy—and connects each one to specific organs in the body. This shows how our emotional health can affect our physical health.

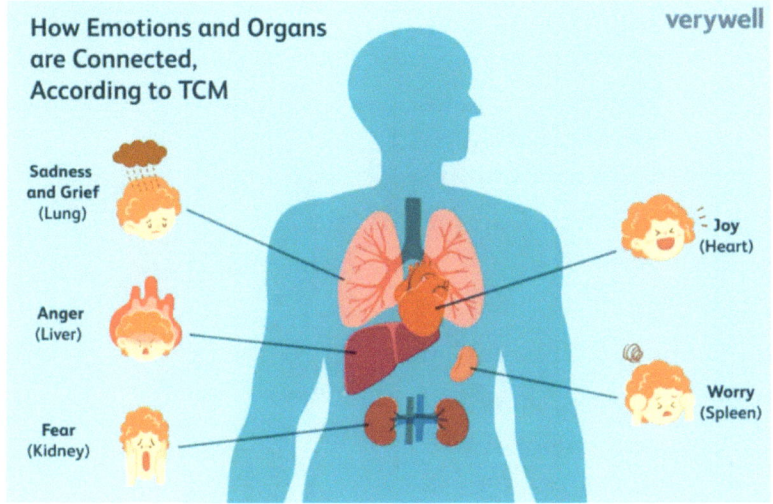

Anger - Liver and Gallbladder

When you experience too much anger—like resentment, irritability, or frustration—it can overwhelm your liver and drain its energy. This imbalance not only affects how you feel emotionally but can also cause physical symptoms like headaches, dizziness, and tension in your neck and shoulders. If you don't address these feelings, it can even raise your risk of high blood pressure and stroke.

Anger is a natural response when things disrupt the liver's functions, which are connected to growth and movement. However, if you let anger build up or keep it bottled inside, it can prevent the liver from doing its job properly, leading to more emotional issues. Anger is closely tied to the liver and gallbladder, and strong emotions like rage can harm the liver over time. If you hold onto anger for too long, it can cause tightness in your gut, shoulders, or jaw, weaken your muscles, and create toxicity in the liver.

Fear - Kidney and Bladder

If fear isn't dealt with, it can seriously harm your kidneys and even lead to problems like kidney stones. When fear becomes a constant presence, especially during life changes or unstable situations, it can greatly impact how your kidneys function. In really intense moments of fright, your kidneys may struggle, which can cause involuntary urination—something many people experience during anxiety-inducing situations like stage fright.

Fear is a natural and primal emotion connected to the kidneys and bladder. While it helps protect us, long-term fear can freeze our responses and weaken not just the kidneys but also the adrenals and nervous system.

Grief - Lungs and Large Intestine

Unresolved grief can cause a range of lung problems, like shallow breathing or shortness of breath. It can also impact the large intestine, increasing the risk of issues like ulcerative colitis.

Grief and sadness can show up in different ways. Many people think of grief as only coming from losing a loved one, but it can also come from any loss, such as changes in relationships, lifestyle, social circles, or work situations. These changes can trigger feelings of grief that affect both our emotional and physical health. When we go through loss, we might experience symptoms like fatigue, colds, and digestive issues. If grief isn't processed over time, it can weaken lung function, making us feel exhausted and affecting how well we breathe.

Worry - Spleen and Stomach
When you think too much or get mentally overstimulated, it can lead to worry, which makes you feel tired and unfocused. Worry is linked to the spleen, an important organ for digestion that helps turn food into nutrients our bodies need. But if you're constantly overthinking and feeling insecure, it can put a strain on the spleen, making it harder for it to do its job.

If the spleen stays weak for a long time, you might feel heavy both physically and emotionally. This can fog your thinking and make it difficult to concentrate, which only adds to your worries. When you struggle to digest what's happening in your life, it can lead to more feelings of exhaustion and mental heaviness, making it even tougher to stay focused.

Joy - Heart and Small intestine
Joy is often seen as just excitement, but it's more than that; true joy brings contentment. While joy connects to the heart and small intestine, too much excitement can cause issues like irritability, trouble sleeping, and heart palpitations. When we feel genuine joy, it nourishes our heart and small intestine, helping us think clearly and process things better. But when we lack joy, it can hurt our heart, leaving us feeling stuck, confused, and having trouble sleeping.

Although it might seem good to always be joyful, too much excitement can actually drain your energy. It's important to keep emotions balanced and experience them in moderation. Short bursts of excitement can be great, but if you stay excited for too long, it can tire you out and deplete your energy reserves. Constantly being expressive without taking time to reflect and rest can feel like a roller coaster, with highs followed by sudden drops, leading to unexpected feelings of sadness.

Another perspective comes from the Western school of thought, which explores emotional energy centers and how these emotions can become lodged in different areas of the body, as illustrated in the diagram below.

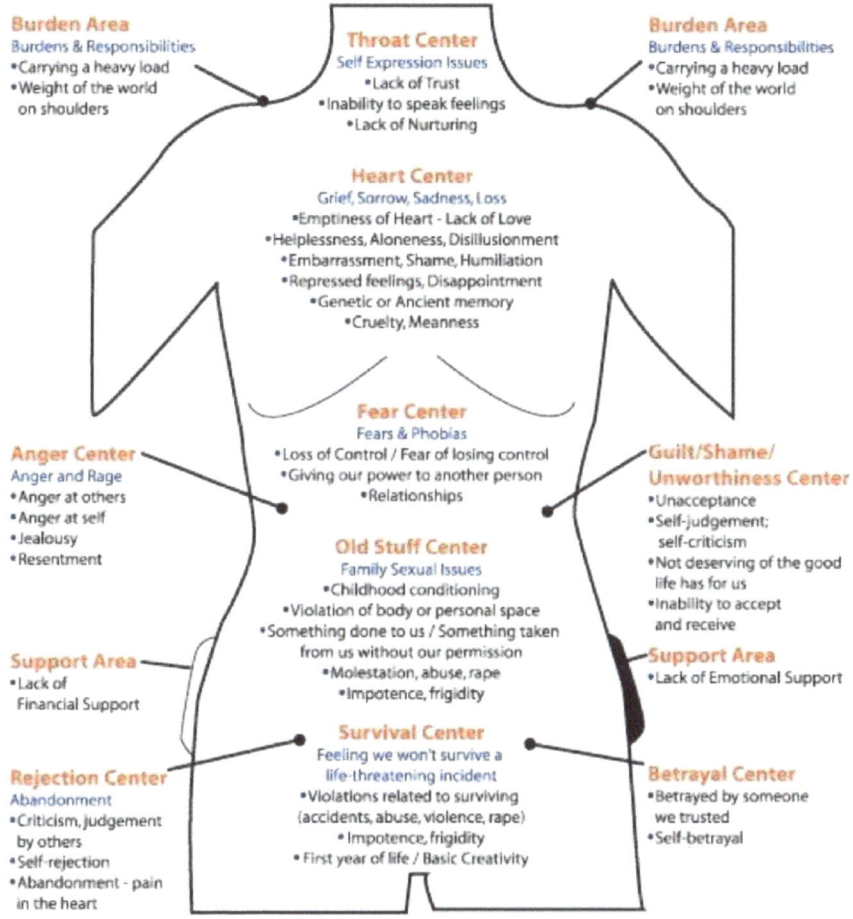

The body stores unresolved or frequently felt emotions in specific organs, where they become lodged. There are 11 emotional centers in the body, each connected to particular emotions and organs. These centers hold the emotional energy, affecting both physical and mental well-being.

It's not just organs. Pain in our body as explained by Josh Richardson, a healer, elaborates about 20 sources of pain in the body that are each directly tied to specific emotional states. According to him, "Pain is first energy, second perception, and third physical manifestation. There is no other source of pain but energy. Physical presentation is always secondary. Every single origin of pain in our bodies can be traced back to a specific emotional state which functions to warn us that there is still work to be done in areas of our lives for which we have yet to integrate lessons. Once we integrate those lessons, the pain disappears.

The body is extremely literal when it comes to pain. The experiences in your life directly manifest in your body and when you encounter an emotional stress, your body shows you exactly what the problem is. The only thing you need to do is decode it."

He further explains the pain experienced in different body parts:

Pain In Your Muscles.
Represents a challenging ability to move in our lives. How flexible we are with our experiences at work, home or within ourselves. Go with the flow.

Pain In Your Head.
Headaches contribute to not making a decision. (Migraines are the daddy of all headaches of knowing what decision to make and not making it.) Be sure to take time out of every day to relax. Do something that eases the tension.

Pain In Your Neck.
Pain in your neck is an indication that you may be having trouble with forgiveness of others, or even yourself. If you're feeling neck pain, consider the things you love about yourself and others. Consciously work toward forgiveness.

EMOTIONAL PAIN CHART

MENTAL THOUGHT PATTERNS THAT FORM OUR EXPERIENCES

Pain Areas and Probable Causes:

Neck: Refusing to see other sides of the question. Stubbornness. Inflexibility.

Shoulders: Represent our ability to carry out experiences in our life joyously. We make life a burden by our attitude.

Spine: Represents the support of life.
- **Upper:** Lack of emotional support. Feeling unloved. Holding back love.
- **Middle:** Guilt. Stuck in the past. Get off my back.
- **Lower:** Fear of money. Lack of financial support.

Elbows: Represents changing directions & accepting new experiences.

Wrists: Represent movement and ease.

Hips: Fear of going forward in major decisions. Nothing to move forward to.

Knees: Stubborn pride and ego. Inability to bend. Fear. Inflexibility. Won't give in.

Ankles: Inflexibility and guilt. Ankles represent the ability to receive pleasure.

Bunions: Lack of joy in meeting experiences in life.

HOW IT WORKS:

"Our body movement is reflective of our inner world." We teach you how to live inside your body. To feel your feet when they strike the ground and know which way you need to turn your foot in order to align your body and work toward being pain-free. It allows you to be conscious in your body while instinctively bringing awareness to your life. Your mind and body have connected. We see this automatically benefit the lives of our clients by helping them make decisions that are in the best interests of their health from choosing better foods to choosing a career that suits them better. A clearer mind helps you to expend less energy everyday and use that energy towards a life you love.

CENTRIPETAL FORCE STUDIO

OTHER CONNECTIONS:

Arthritis: Feeling unloved. Criticism. Resentment.

Bone Breaks/Fractures: Rebelling against authority.

Bursitis: Repressed anger.

Inflammation: Fear. Seeing red. Inflamed thinking.

Joint Pain: Represent changes in direction in life and the ease of these movements.

Loss of Balance: Not centered. Scattered thinking.

Sciatica: Being hypocritical. Fear of money and or the future.

Slipped Disc: Indecisive. Feeling totally unsupported by life.

Sprains: Not wanting to move in a certain direction in life. Anger and resistance.

Stiffness: Rigid, stiff thinking.

Weakness: A need for mental rest.

CENTRIPETAL FORCE: sen-trip-i-tl: a pathway to the center | fohrs: physical power or strength possessed by a living being

Information from Heal Your Body A-Z by Louise L. Hay

Pain In Your Gums.
Like the neck, pain in the gums is attributed to not making a decision for yourself and not sticking to it if you did. Be clear, and go for it!

Pain In Your Shoulders.
Pain in your shoulders may indicate that you're carrying a real emotional burden. That's where the saying "shouldering a problem" comes from. Focus on some proactive problem solving and distributing some of that burden to other people in your life.

Pain In Your Stomach.
Carries recognition of digesting life, or not. GI distress is about not feeling fulfilled, leaving a hole and causing grief.

Pain In Your Upper Back.
If you're feeling pain in your upper back, you're probably coping with a lack of emotional support. You might be feeling unloved or you could even be holding your love back. If you're single, it might be time to go for a date.

Pain In Your Lower Back.
Lower back pain might mean you're worrying too much about money or you're lacking in emotional support. It may be a good time to ask for an overdue raise or consider a financial planner to help you utilize money a little bit better.

Pain In Your Sacrum and Tail Bone.
You may be sitting on an issue that needs to be addressed. Get to the bottom of it and you will see resolution.

Pain In Your Elbows.
Pain in your elbows has a lot to do with resisting changes in your life. If your arms are feeling stiff, it may mean that you're too stiff

in your life. It may be time to think about making compromises and shaking things up a little bit. At the very least, go with the flow.

Pain In Your Arms In General.
You're carrying something or someone as an emotional burden. It may be time to ask yourself why do you keep carrying it?

Pain In Your Hands.
With your hands, you reach out to others and connect. If you're feeling hand pain, it may mean that you're not reaching out enough. Try making new friends. Have lunch with an associate. Make a connection. It may also represent holding or letting go.

Pain In Your Hips.
If you've been afraid of moving, that may manifest as a pain in the hips. Sore hips could be a sign that you're too resistant to changes and moves. It may also show a caution toward making decisions. If you're thinking on some big ideas, it's time to make a decision. General pain in the hips relates to support. When they slip out, it generally relates to an imbalance in how you are relating to life. Feeling the lack of love and support.

Pain In Your Joints In General.
Like muscles, pain in joints represents flexibility or lack of situations and your attachments to them. Be open-minded to new thoughts, lessons and experiences.

Pain In the Knees.
Seeing life as unsupported. Inside knee; community, job, friends. Outside knee; personal issues. Humble yourself. Spend some time volunteering. Make sure you remember that you're mortal. You're just human and although you have an ego, don't let it rule over your life.

Pain In Your Teeth.
Not liking your situation and repeating that dislike in your thoughts and emotions daily. Repeat to yourself that experiences are flowing through easily as you integrate perceived positive or negative experiences with ease.

Pain In Your Ankles.
Pain in your ankles may be a sign that you're depriving yourself of pleasure. It may mean it's time to indulge a little bit more. Spice up your romantic life a bit.

Pain Causing Fatigue.
Boredom, resistance, and denying what it takes to move forward. Ask yourself, "What's next?" Open yourself to that little voice which speaks very softly and nudges you towards a new experience.

Pain In Your Feet.
When you're depressed, you might feel some foot pain. Too much negativity can manifest in your feet not feeling so good. Look for the little joys in life. Find a new pet or a new hobby. Look for joy.

Pain That Is Unexplained In Different Body Parts.
The cellular structure is currently being recorded in the human body and in the process, it is purging and letting go of predominant resident frequencies that are being eliminated. For this energy to clear, the immune system and actually all systems within the body must be effectively weakened. So while the body may appear to be in a state of illness, it is more or less in a state of clearing. Know that it will pass.

We are emotional beings, and it's natural for us to express our feelings openly. However, many people learn to hide their emotions, especially the negative ones, instead of figuring out how to express them healthily. This can make it hard to deal with and release trauma from our lives.

Just like a backpack becomes heavier with each added item, our bodies can feel weighed down by unprocessed emotions. Carrying this emotional baggage affects our overall well-being and impacts our organs and health. Everyone experiences trauma, whether big or small. If we don't allow ourselves to feel and express the emotions tied to these experiences, they can become trapped within us. Over time, these emotions can drain our energy, create imbalances, and lead to physical issues. Continuously suppressing our feelings can build up toxicity in our body, mind, and heart, ultimately harming our health and happiness.

Happiness can be pursued, engineered and bought.
Joy needs to be uncovered and realised, inside.

- Indroneil

Chapter 4
About Bach Flower Remedies

INTRO TO BACH FLOWER REMEDIES

Bach Flower essences are quantum medicines.
Derived from the essences of flower of wild trees and bushes and unlike essential oils or herbal extracts that contain the physical substances extracted from plants, there is no physical, chemical or biochemical component of the flower left in a flower essence. Instead, the life-force and vibrational signature of the flower is imprinted within a water-based matrix. This makes healing and transforming with Bach essences, absolutely safe, simple and without any side effects.

The impact of flower essences
Flower essences do not operate through biochemical intervention but through resonance in the subtle human energy field. Unlike pharmaceuticals or some herbal medicines, flower essences do not suppress symptoms but work through vibrational energetics. They stimulate all five bodies of human existence, addressing physical and emotional health. Flower essences aim to raise awareness levels and restore individuals to homeostasis and harmony. Their impact is rooted in vibrational energetics rather than biochemical processes.

Healing Emotional States and Beyond
There are 38 unique Bach flower essences that address 38 unique emotional states. These essences can be combined to create millions of composites, which heal the complex and dynamic clusters of human emotions and thus almost all conceivable mental and emotional conditions and even physical conditions that arise out of their repression.

As the flower essences are absolutely safe and without any side effects, they may be used to self-medicate and get temporary relief. However, to be able to heal irreversibly from the root, it is essential to seek help of a competent practitioner who understands the interplay of human emotions, can delve into the unconscious to get to the root cause and knows how to create 'harmonious composites' that heal holistically.

History of Bach Flowers Remedies
Dr. Edward Bach was born in 1886, in Moseley, England. He began his medical career by studying at University College Hospital in London from 1906 to 1912. After finishing his training, he worked as a doctor, and by 1922, he had a general practice on Harley Street. During his career, he also learned about bacteriology, immunology, and homeopathy, which deepened his understanding of health.

As he treated patients, Dr. Bach noticed that people reacted differently to illnesses. This made him realize that true healing should look at the person as a whole, not just the physical symptoms. Frustrated with how conventional medicine focused mainly on diseases, he believed there had to be a more natural way to heal. So, in the late 1920s, he left his successful practice to create a new system of healing using non-toxic plants and flowers.

By the 1920s, Dr. Bach was convinced that our emotions play a big role in our health. He started searching for natural remedies that could help with emotional issues and began to explore the healing properties of flowers. He believed that each flower had a unique energy that could help restore emotional balance.

Between 1928 and 1935, he developed 38 remedies, each designed to target specific emotional states like fear, loneliness, and stress. For example, he created Mimulus for specific fears and Aspen for more vague anxieties. He also made Rescue Remedy, a blend that helps reduce stress and provides comfort in emergencies. His holistic approach highlighted the link between mind and body, suggesting that by addressing emotional problems, people could also improve their physical health. This idea was quite groundbreaking for his time.

In 1934, Dr. Bach shared his belief about healing, saying that it happens "not by attacking the disease, but by filling our bodies with the uplifting vibrations of our Higher Nature, allowing illness to fade away like snow in the sun." He believed that real healing involves changing how we see things, leading to peace of mind and inner happiness.

That same year, he moved to a small house called Mount Vernon in Sotwell, Oxfordshire. In this peaceful place, he found the last 19 remedies, drawing inspiration from the beautiful garden and nature around him. Once he completed the set, he felt satisfied that his work was done.

Dr. Bach famously said in 1931, "The dawn of a new and better art of healing is upon us," showing his hope for a new approach to health. He passed away in 1936, feeling confident that he had created a simple way for people to heal themselves, covering a wide range of human emotions and moods.

How Bach Flower Remedies are made

The remedies are created using two primary methods: the sun method and the boiling method. The sun method, designed for delicate flowers, involves floating fully open blooms in pure spring water for three hours under direct sunlight, a process known as solarization, which allows the flowers' energy to infuse into the water.

For sturdier plants, the boiling method is applied, where the flowering parts are boiled for half an hour. This heat extracts the essence, which is mixed with brandy to create the mother tincture.

Once prepared, the mother tincture is diluted at a ratio of two drops to 30 ml of brandy to create the stock bottles found in stores. Making these remedies is straightforward and requires only the right plant, sunshine, and water.

Dr. Bach emphasized the importance of not handling the flowers directly, ensuring that their energy influences the remedy. On a sunny day, you fill a glass bowl with spring water and gently place the flowers on the surface. This process fosters a calming experience, encouraging gratitude for the plants used in the creation of the remedies.

Bach Flowers Remedies
Dr. Edward Bach discovered a total of 38 remedies during his quest for natural healing solutions, of which 37 are derived from flowers, while one is sourced from rock water. Each of these remedies was designed to address specific emotional states and mental conditions, reflecting.

Agrimony
"Behind my smile, there's a lot I don't share."

Agrimony is for those who hide their worries behind a cheerful exterior while struggling with inner turmoil. Often seen as the life of the party, these individuals use humor to mask their true feelings but dislike being alone. When distractions fade, the repressed pain becomes overwhelming, and many may turn to alcohol or drugs to maintain their facade of happiness.

This remedy encourages individuals to confront the darker aspects of their lives, helping them to become more well-rounded. While it doesn't take away their sense of humour, Agrimony teaches that laughter can acknowledge and dispel troubles rather than hide from them. It guides those who rely on jokes and false smiles to face painful realities and find true emotional well-being.

Aspen

"I feel anxious for no reason at all."

You feel on edge but can't say why. Aspen is the remedy for unexplained anxiety and fear, often accompanied by physical sensations like trembling, sweating, or butterflies in the stomach. This remedy addresses the nameless fears that can range from a vague sense of foreboding to intense terror, leaving individuals feeling uneasy without understanding the cause.

Though some associate Aspen with nighttime fears, such as dreams or night terrors, it is essential to note that these nameless anxieties can arise at any time, even in broad daylight. While Aspen helps to alleviate this unconscious anxiety, its positive potential lies in fostering fearlessness and reducing apprehension, allowing individuals to face life with greater confidence.

Beech

"I often catch myself judging others too harshly."

Beech is the remedy for those who easily become irritated and struggle to accept differences in others. Often valuing order and precision, individuals in a Beech state may find it hard to understand why not everyone lives by their standards.

Described by Dr. Bach as a remedy for those who need to see more goodness and beauty in their surroundings, Beech encourages compassion and understanding. As individuals begin to embrace tolerance, their irritability fades, allowing them to appreciate the unique paths others are on and recognize that everyone is striving for their own version of perfection.

Centaury

"I have trouble saying no to people."

Centaury is the remedy for those who struggle to assert themselves, often yielding to others' wishes and neglecting their own needs. These kind, gentle souls may feel bound by familial duty or a desire to help, but this often leads to being taken advantage of rather than being a willing servant.

Instead of hardening their hearts, the Centaury remedy fosters courage and self-determination, empowering individuals to stand up for themselves. It helps create healthy boundaries, allowing them to make space for their own desires and needs while still being compassionate towards others.

Cerato

"I often doubt my own judgment."

Cerato is the remedy for those who lack confidence in their decisions, often needing external validation before moving forward. This constant quest for approval can lead to missed opportunities, as individuals become talkative, asking endless questions that can drain the energy of those around them.

While they may make decisions easily, doubts quickly creep in afterward, leaving them unsure of their choices. Cerato encourages individuals to cultivate faith in their judgment, helping them listen to their inner voice and trust their intuition. As confidence grows, they become more self-reliant and wiser, able to navigate their path without relying on the opinions of others.

Cherry Plum

"I fear losing control of my emotions."

Cherry Plum is the remedy for those who experience intense fear of losing self-control, often feeling like a ticking time bomb on the verge of an emotional breakdown. This state can lead to uncontrolled outbursts of rage, leaving individuals worried they might harm themselves or others.

Dr. Bach categorised Cherry Plum under the umbrella of Fear, as it specifically addresses the anxiety of acting irrationally or going mad. It is also beneficial for those who have already lost control, as it helps calm the frantic fear associated with such moments. Much like the fear a small child feels during a tantrum, Cherry Plum offers support and courage, enabling individuals to regain their composure in crisis situations. This remedy is even part of Dr. Bach's original crisis formula, designed for emergency use.

Chestnut Bud

"I keep making the same mistakes."

Chestnut Bud is the remedy for those who struggle to learn from past experiences, often rushing into new situations without applying the lessons they should have gained. This pattern can manifest in various ways, such as a person who repeatedly falls for the same type of partner or takes on identical jobs, only to feel unfulfilled each time.

While it's healthy to move on from the past, individuals in a Chestnut Bud state may do so without reflecting on their experiences, leading them to repeat the same errors. This remedy fosters better insight, observation, and wisdom, allowing individuals to genuinely learn from their past and embrace truly new experiences rather than falling into familiar patterns of failure.

Chicory

"I tend to be possessive of my loved ones."

Chicory is the remedy for individuals who care deeply for their families and friends but expect constant attention and love in return. This possessive love can become overwhelming, leading to feelings of hurt and resentment when their expectations are not met. Often, those in a Chicory state may try to "over-manage" their loved ones' lives, which can stifle their growth and independence.

While their intentions stem from love, this behaviour can drive people away rather than draw them closer. Chicory helps transform this possessiveness into selfless love, encouraging individuals to give without expecting anything in return. By fostering unconditional love and allowing others the freedom to grow, Chicory nurtures healthier, more fulfilling relationships.

Clematis

"I often daydream and lose touch with reality."

Clematis is the remedy for those whose minds drift away from the present, lost in their own imagination and dreaming of future successes or creative pursuits. While this imaginative state can be a source of inspiration, it often leads to absentmindedness and a lack of grounding in reality, making it challenging to turn dreams into actions.

Individuals in a Clematis state may find themselves withdrawn, prone to drowsiness, and easily distracted by their thoughts. This remedy helps bring them back to reality, encouraging them to engage with the present and take steps toward building a fulfilling life. Clematis encourages a vibrant interest in the here and now. As one of the ingredients in Dr. Bach's original crisis formula, it aids those feeling light-headed or fuzzy, providing clarity and focus in moments of emergency.

Crab Apple

"I feel unclean or uncomfortable in my own skin."

Known as the cleansing remedy, Crab Apple is for those who struggle with feelings of uncleanliness or self-loathing, often fixating on a specific flaw in their appearance or personality. This remedy addresses self-hatred and can manifest as obsessive behaviours related to hygiene or an overwhelming concern about being contaminated.

Individuals in a Crab Apple state may become preoccupied with minor imperfections, sometimes overlooking more significant issues in their lives. By promoting acceptance and control over their thoughts, Crab Apple helps individuals cleanse obsessive behaviours, allowing them to embrace their true selves without judgment. It is also considered an important ingredient in the cream version of Dr. Bach's original crisis formula, serving to restore balance and self-acceptance.

Elm

"I feel overwhelmed by my responsibilities."

Elm is the remedy for individuals who experience a temporary loss of confidence due to the weight of their responsibilities. Typically, strong and capable leaders, these individuals may suddenly feel inadequate and exhausted under pressure, struggling to keep up with their commitments.

While they are usually successful in their endeavours, the burden of their responsibilities can sometimes feel overwhelming. Elm helps dispel feelings of inadequacy, allowing individuals to regain their confidence and efficiency. Unlike Larch types, who doubt their abilities from the outset and often avoid challenges, Elm individuals willingly take on tasks but may momentarily feel overwhelmed by their scale. This remedy supports them in resuming their lives without the fear of failure, enabling them to embrace their capabilities once more.

Gentian

"I get discouraged easily."

Gentian is the remedy for those who experience mild feelings of downheartedness following specific disappointments, such as failing a job interview, facing redundancy, or dealing with a breakup. While these feelings of negativity and pessimism may arise, individuals often maintain a glimmer of hope, ready to try again despite their temporary loss of confidence.

This remedy helps lift the weight of discouragement, allowing individuals to regain their positive outlook more quickly. Those in a Gentian state are more willing to bounce back and make another attempt. Gentian supports a proactive approach, helping to overcome setbacks and embrace the possibility of success once more.

Gorse

"I've lost hope and feel defeated."

Gorse is the remedy for individuals who experience profound feelings of downheartedness, believing there is no light at the end of the tunnel. This state represents a stronger version of despair than Gentian, as those in a Gorse state have often given up hope and refuse to be encouraged, convinced that their situation is hopeless.

People suffering from Gorse may think they are incurable if they are ill, feeling that nothing can be done to improve their circumstances. Dr. Bach classified Gorse as a remedy for uncertainty rather than outright despair, highlighting that the core issue is often a loss of faith. Gorse helps individuals shift their perspective, allowing them to regain hope, faith, and strength from within, and guiding them toward a more positive outlook and potential solutions.

Heather

"I need attention and find it hard to be alone."

Heather is the remedy for individuals who are overly focused on themselves, often monopolising conversations and finding it difficult to be alone. These individuals tend to talk extensively about their problems, great and small, making them poor listeners with little interest in others' issues. This self-obsession can lead to loneliness, as others may start to avoid them.

Dr. Bach referred to these individuals as "buttonholers" because they latch onto people, seeking an audience for their concerns. The Heather remedy helps shift this focus, allowing individuals to recognise the importance of others' experiences. As they learn to listen and engage with compassion, they become more approachable, fostering genuine connections instead of driving people away. This transformation enables them to create meaningful relationships built on empathy rather than self-centeredness.

Holly

"I feel angry or jealous towards others."

Holly is the remedy for individuals experiencing strong negative emotions, including anger, jealousy, resentment, and a desire for revenge. These feelings can lead to outbursts of temper and aggressive behaviour, making it difficult to find inner peace.

While Holly is often associated with anger, it addresses deeper issues of hatred, suspicion, and envy directed at others. The core problem in a Holly state is a lack of love, and this remedy aims to foster goodwill and generosity of spirit. By encouraging openness and compassion towards others, Holly helps individuals transform their negative emotions into a more harmonious and loving outlook.

Honeysuckle

"I keep thinking of the good old days."

Honeysuckle is the remedy for those who find themselves reminiscing about better days gone by, often feeling regret for missed opportunities or longing for the "good old days." This state is common among individuals in middle or old age, as well as those experiencing grief, divorce, or the aftermath of failed ventures.

People in a Honeysuckle state believe their best days are behind them, which can lead to a sense of nostalgia or homesickness. This remedy encourages individuals to cherish their past happiness while letting go of it, allowing them to fully engage with the present and look forward to the future. Honeysuckle helps us learn from our experiences without being trapped by them, enabling a joyful embrace of today and tomorrow.

Hornbeam

"I often feel worn out before the day even begins."

Hornbeam is the remedy for individuals who experience a lack of motivation and feel exhausted at the prospect of upcoming tasks, often reminiscent of a "Monday morning feeling." This state brings doubts about one's strength or ability to cope, leading to procrastination and an aversion to menial tasks.

Those in a Hornbeam state may find it easier to stay in bed or engage in distractions rather than face the demands of the day. However, once they muster the effort to begin, the weariness typically dissipates, showing that this fatigue is largely mental rather than stemming from actual exhaustion. Hornbeam helps lift spirits and restore confidence, enabling individuals to tackle their responsibilities with renewed energy and a sense of capability.

Impatiens

"I struggle with impatience and get frustrated easily."

Impatiens is the remedy for those who experience frustration and irritability due to their desire for everything to be done quickly. Individuals in this state often have more active minds and can become restless, leading to mental tension from the frustration of waiting or dealing with slower-paced individuals.

Those who resonate with Impatiens tend to finish others' sentences or prefer to complete tasks themselves to avoid the irritation of waiting. This remedy encourages patience, helping individuals to slow down and adopt a more relaxed attitude toward life. Impatiens is also an ingredient in Dr. Bach's original crisis formula, where it serves to calm agitated thoughts and feelings, promoting a sense of ease and understanding in interactions with others.

Larch

"I often feel unsure about my abilities."

Larch is the remedy for individuals who feel inferior to others and struggle to believe in themselves. Often convinced of their impending failure, they may not even attempt new challenges, reinforcing their feelings of inadequacy.

Larch helps individuals move forward despite their fears of success or failure, encouraging them to take risks and engage more fully in life. By fostering confidence in their abilities, Larch empowers individuals to embrace opportunities and gain a richer, more rewarding experience.

Mimulus

"I often find myself anxious about specific things."

Mimulus is the remedy for individuals who experience anxiety related to known fears, such as public speaking, illness, money issues, or even the fear of death. It addresses everyday fears that can cause significant discomfort and may also be associated with shyness, nervousness, and tendencies to blush or stammer.

This remedy is particularly effective for phobias when the specific source of fear—be it spiders, heights, or aggressive dogs—can be named. Mimulus helps individuals confront their specific anxieties and face their fears with courage. By fostering a sense of strength and resilience, Mimulus enables individuals to navigate life's challenges without irrational worry.

Mustard

"I feel a heavy cloud of sadness for no clear reason."

Mustard is the remedy for individuals experiencing deep gloom and depression that seems to appear out of nowhere, often described as a heaviness weighing down the spirit. Those in this state may feel enveloped in darkness, with reduced energy and a lack of joy, despite having no apparent reason for their melancholy.

Even when they recognise the reasons for happiness in their lives, everything may still seem black and hopeless. Mustard helps lift this pervasive sadness, dispelling the clouds of gloom and allowing individuals to reconnect with inner serenity and joy, creating a sense of lightness that cannot be easily shaken.

Oak

"I push through challenges, even when I'm completely worn out."

Oak is the remedy for strong, resilient individuals who push through adversity without recognising their need for rest. These determined people often carry a heavy sense of duty and responsibility, feeling frustrated when illness or exhaustion forces them to slow down.

While their bravery and perseverance are admirable, they may ignore their body's natural signals for rest, risking chronic exhaustion. Oak helps individuals understand their limits and encourages them to embrace the importance of self-care. This remedy fosters the strength to remain stable under pressure while teaching the vital lesson that sometimes letting go is necessary to avoid breaking under strain.

Olive

"I am totally exhausted."

Olive is the remedy for individuals who have reached their breaking point, often expressing feelings of complete fatigue after prolonged periods of strain, such as a long illness, severe sleep deprivation, caring for a loved one, or maintaining a poor diet. This exhaustion leaves them feeling weak and lacking zest for life, with every task feeling like an uphill battle.

Olive focuses on restoring strength after hard work or mental strain. This remedy helps replenish energy and instills the faith needed to continue moving forward. With Olive, individuals can either feel revitalised or finally achieve the restful sleep they desperately need, allowing them to regain a sense of balance and well-being.

Pine

"I often blame myself for things that go wrong."

Pine is the remedy for individuals who struggle with self-blame and guilt, often apologising even when they have done nothing wrong. Those in a Pine state frequently feel that they could have performed better, leading to a constant sense of dissatisfaction with their efforts.

This remedy addresses the unnecessary guilt that can arise from taking on responsibility for things outside of one's control or even mistakes made by others. Individuals may find themselves excessively saying "sorry" and punishing themselves for perceived shortcomings. Pine helps cultivate a balanced approach to responsibility, allowing individuals to acknowledge their faults without becoming consumed by them. It empowers them to correct mistakes when possible while recognising their limits, leading to a sense of contentment when they have truly done their best.

Red Chestnut

"I worry too much about my loved ones."

Red Chestnut is the remedy for individuals who feel excessive worry for the well-being of others, such as a husband fretting over his wife's safety at night or a mother anxious about her child at school. While these concerns stem from love, they can become overwhelming, leading to negative and harmful thoughts that undermine the confidence of those they care about.

This remedy addresses the natural fears that become magnified to the point of affecting relationships negatively. Red Chestnut helps individuals maintain calm and perspective, allowing them to send out reassuring and unworried thoughts to their loved ones. By fostering a sense of stability and support, individuals can be a source of strength for others, instead of contributing to their anxiety.

Rock Rose

"When fear takes over, I feel completely paralysed."

Rock Rose is the remedy for individuals experiencing intense fear and panic, often accompanied by physical symptoms like trembling or sweating. This state may arise suddenly, escalating anxieties that can feel very real, even if they are not always rational. It is particularly useful for those dealing with nightmares or panic attacks.

As an important component of Dr. Bach's traditional crisis combination, Rock Rose addresses the terror that can overshadow more everyday fears. When in a Rock Rose state, conscious thought and decision-making become nearly impossible due to the overwhelming panic. This remedy helps restore calm and courage, enabling individuals to move beyond their fears and embrace a sense of fearlessness.

Rock Water

"I'm too hard on myself and need to lighten up."

Rock Water is the remedy for individuals who impose strict standards on themselves and others, often leading to self-repression and denial of enjoyable experiences. Those in this state can be harsh and critical, both of themselves and of those who do not meet their high ideals, resulting in a rigid and inflexible approach to life.

While they strive for perfection and seek to be exemplary figures for others. Rock Water allows individuals to maintain their ideals without the weight of self-punishment. This remedy promotes flexibility and self-compassion, encouraging a kinder attitude toward themselves and a greater appreciation for life's simpler pleasures.

Scleranthus

"I struggle to make decisions and often feel unsure."

Scleranthus is the remedy for individuals who face uncertainty and indecision, often over trivial matters. This state can lead to inner restlessness, difficulty concentrating, and an inability to order thoughts and impulses, ultimately consuming energy without achieving anything.

Scleranthus helps clarify thoughts and emotions. Scleranthus can also manifest through mood swings or even motion sickness, as the core issue remains indecision. By taking this remedy, individuals can reconnect with their intuition, enabling them to make decisions quickly and confidently, leading to a more decisive and purposeful life.

Star of Bethlehem

"I feel troubled by past traumas."

Star of Bethlehem is the remedy for individuals dealing with the after-effects of shock, grief, or trauma caused by unexpected events such as loss, accidents, or disturbing news. This remedy addresses inner numbness, paralysing sorrow, and the lingering impacts of past traumas that may affect present circumstances.

As one of the remedies in the traditional crisis formula, Star of Bethlehem can provide comfort and soothing to those experiencing emotional pain, whether from recent events or traumas that occurred long ago, even in childhood. It is particularly effective for feelings of emptiness and loss that arise when a loved one dies or moves away. By offering solace, this remedy helps individuals begin to heal and find peace amid their sorrow.

Sweet Chestnut

"I feel like I'm at the end of my rope."

Sweet Chestnut is the remedy for individuals who feel they have reached the limits of their endurance, grappling with profound mental despair and a sense of hopelessness. These individuals have explored all avenues and see no possible solutions, feeling utterly helpless and vulnerable in their acute state of emergency.

Individuals experiencing Sweet Chestnut are at the end of their rope, facing deep despair. This remedy provides essential support, helping them regain mastery over their lives and renew hope and strength. Often, it opens up new possibilities, reminding individuals that even in their darkest moments, a way forward may emerge when they least expect it.

Vervain

"I can be too intense or overly enthusiastic."

Vervain is for people who are very enthusiastic and have a strong sense of justice. They often become perfectionists, taking on too much work and feeling stressed out because they can't relax. Their passion can be contagious, but sometimes it turns into fanaticism, making it hard for them to listen to other viewpoints.

When in this state, Vervain helps people find balance and calm their busy minds. It encourages them to relax and accept that others may have different opinions. This remedy helps them enjoy life more and appreciate the passing of time instead of always feeling the need to stay busy and active.

Vine

"I often try to control others too much."

Vine is for people who are strong leaders and often think they know what's best for others. While they have powerful energy, their desire for control can lead them to dominate others forcefully. This can make them seem aggressive and overly demanding, expecting complete obedience without caring much about others' feelings.

Negative examples of Vine include tyrannical fathers or overbearing bosses who focus on getting their orders followed. In a positive light, Vine individuals can become wise and understanding leaders who inspire and guide others gently, without needing to impose their will. When someone falls into the habit of giving orders, this remedy helps them tap into their ability to lead with kindness and wisdom.

Walnut

"I have a hard time adapting to change."

Walnut is the remedy for individuals who struggle to adjust during transitions in life, such as puberty, marriage, having children, starting a new job, or retirement. It also helps those who might be swayed from their life path by more dominant personalities or find it hard to let go of the past.

Walnut people may find themselves influenced by opinions offered to them, leading to doubt about their path. This remedy supports individuals in navigating life's transitions, helping them break ties with the past and adjust more easily to new stages in life while protecting them from external influences.

Water Violet

"I prefer to keep to myself and feel distant from others."

Water Violet is the remedy for individuals who are talented and capable but often come across as distant or unapproachable due to their preference for solitude. These individuals are typically quiet and dignified, enjoying their own company or the company of a few close friends.

While their independence is admirable, it can create emotional barriers that lead to loneliness and difficulty connecting with others. Water Violet helps break down these barriers, encouraging individuals to open up and engage more with the world around them. This remedy fosters a sense of balance, allowing them to become more involved with humanity and enrich their relationships while still valuing their need for solitude.

White Chestnut

"I can't stop my mind from racing with thoughts."

White Chestnut is the remedy for those who experience intrusive thoughts and mental arguments that prevent them from concentrating. These thoughts can feel relentless, replaying in the mind like a looped recording, leading to exhaustion and difficulty finding peace.

While often described as "worrying," White Chestnut thoughts are not necessarily filled with anxiety; instead, they are more repetitive and unproductive. This remedy helps clear the mind, allowing individuals to think straight and address any underlying issues calmly and rationally. It can also be beneficial for insomnia, providing a natural way to promote restful sleep and mental clarity.

Wild Oat

"I'm unsure about my direction in life."

Wild Oat is the remedy for individuals who have ambition and a desire to achieve something meaningful but struggle to identify what that is. They often drift from one endeavour to another, feeling frustrated and bored when none bring them true happiness.

Individuals may know they want a fulfilling life but are uncertain whether that means getting married, finding a career, or changing religions. Wild Oat helps clarify these options, reconnecting individuals with their sense of purpose and guiding them toward their true path in life, making the way ahead feel more attainable.

Wild Rose

"I feel apathetic and resigned to my situation."

Wild Rose is the remedy for individuals who feel resigned to their circumstances, lacking vitality and purpose. They may accept whatever life throws at them without complaint, often failing to recognize their role in creating positive change. This easygoing attitude can lead to a sense of apathy, where there is little motivation to engage with the world or pursue fulfilment.

In this state, people drift along without actively seeking improvement in their lives. Wild Rose helps to reawaken their interest in life, encouraging a shift from apathy to enthusiasm. In a positive Wild Rose state, individuals experience a renewed sense of purpose, bringing increased happiness and enjoyment to their everyday experiences.

Willow

"I often feel bitter about my circumstances."

Willow is the remedy for individuals who feel bitter about their circumstances, often blaming others for their misfortunes. They may carry grudges and feel sulky, leading to negative thoughts like "Life can be so unfair." This mindset can create a cycle of self-pity and resentment towards others' successes.

In this state, individuals struggle to recognise their own accomplishments and tend to focus on what they lack. Willow helps to foster a sense of optimism and encourages individuals to take full responsibility for their fate. By promoting generosity towards others and awareness of how negative thinking can attract further misfortune, this remedy supports a shift towards a more positive outlook on life.

Rescue Remedy

"I need calm and comfort in stressful situations."

Rescue Remedy, also known as the crisis formula, is a blend of five different flower essences, Cherry Plum, Clematis, Impatiens, Rock Rose, and Star of Bethlehem, designed to provide quick relief in moments of crisis, acute stress or emotional emergency.

Rescue Remedy promotes a sense of calm and reassurance, helping you to regain your composure and focus. It encourages emotional balance, making it easier to navigate challenging situations with a clear mind.

Dr. Bach's approach was innovative for his time, as he focused not just on treating physical symptoms but also on nurturing the emotional aspects of health. He emphasized that healing begins with the mind and spirit, and these remedies serve as a gentle means to achieve that balance. The complete set of 38 remedies reflects Bach's holistic philosophy, providing a comprehensive toolkit for emotional healing and personal growth.

5 Reasons Why Back Flower Therapy is Preferred for Mental and Emotional Well-being

Nothing can be more revolutionary in the history of wellness than the advent of Bach Flower Remedies (BFR). Discovered between 1920s and 30s by the Harley Street, British physician, Dr. Edward Bach, it's a system of 38 remedies prepared using the essence of 38 wild flowers and flowers of wild trees and shrubs.

Considered to be a New Age complementary and alternative medicine (CAM) system, Bach Flower Remedies along with 4 million-plus possible combinations are being used currently in over 70 countries world over. Bach flower therapy is particularly popular amongst the celebrities in the West.

Here are 5 reasons why Bach Flower therapy is a preferred therapy for mental and emotional well-being:

- Bach Flower remedies contain no bio-chemic component and are purely energetic in nature, hence can be used as a complementary therapy alongside any other course of treatment with no danger of side-effects, over-dosing or contra-indications. They are non-toxic, non-addictive and gluten free and spare mankind from the scourge of side effects and damages that are alleged to be caused by contemporary medicine. The remedies can be used on babies, expectant mothers, children, adults, aged people, pets and even plants.

- Each of the 38 remedies address specific mental / emotional blocks. These can be combined to create more than 4 million composites, that can heal almost all conceivable mental and emotional challenges. Besides addressing day to day issues and restoring harmony, Bach Flower remedies addresses mental health issues like Addiction, Anger, Anxiety, Depression, Fears and Phobias, Grief, Impatience, Lack of self-confidence and self-esteem, Loneliness, Low self-worth, Mental exhaustion, PTSD, Relationship issues, Sleeplessness, Stress, Suicidal tendencies, and Trauma, among others.

- Bach Flower therapy can not only heal an individual of diseases but completely transform. Able therapists administer remedies that heal in layers starting from negative thoughts, feelings and behaviours; habits and attitudes and finally deep-seated beliefs and conditionings - the root cause. This leads to permanent healing of the whole 'being' and irreversible inner transformation.

- Bach Flower therapy heals the body of consciousness – the Wisdom body or Vigyanmaya Kosha (the 4th level of existence) according to Patanjali's theory of Panchakoshas – the five levels of human existence - dissolving blocks in the sub conscious and aligning all the other sub ordinate bodies to a state of wholeness and harmony. As the healing happens at the 4th level of human existence, that is the Wisdom body, it heals holistically the mind body, the energy body and even the physical body. Thus, Bach flower therapy is useful in healing diseases like joint problems, asthma, auto immune disorders, diabetes and hypertension, among others. Even neurological disorders like insomnia, Parkinsonism, Alzheimer's etc. can be effectively treated by these remedies.

- Bach Flower therapy is simple and subtle. It does not need any material or personal intervention. The flowers do the healing. For all modalities working at lower levels of human consciousness, for example the likes of Ayurveda, Reiki, Pranic Healing, Homeopathy and Acupuncture somebody, something else, some agent has to be involved in the healing process. On which one is dependent. This 'other' casts a shadow on the 'being', no matter what the quality of this shadow is. Bach flower therapy makes you perfectly conscious without any shadow, any dependence, absolute light with no darkness. There is no material input … only vibrational … and that to subtle signature vibrations of 38 blessed flowers of higher order… natural, pure, innocent, simple and gentle.

Bach Flower therapy is fast emerging as the future medicine, because if just by healing the consciousness, the mind, the vital body and the gross body can be healed, then why depend on toxic chemicals and dependence-creating modalities, why not work it through the power of consciousness?

Evolution of Bach Flower Therapy & Floral Alchemy™

Bach Flower remedies have been around for close to a hundred years now. During this time, several practitioners have dabbled with them in their pursuit to address/ heal certain human conditions. In the absence of specific guidelines for practice, several approaches have prevailed. With more and more wisdom being derivedfrom experience with clients and the same getting ploughedback into the practice, the approach to practice has evolved.

If we closely look at the evolutionary trend, we shall clearly see three stages of evolution.

Stage One – Fixing Symptoms
This is the stage where the practitioner would simplistically map remedies to symptoms from the repertory of tools, often alleviating the symptom. Few practitioners would advise just one remedy. He or she

would not investigate much to uncover the condition underlying the symptoms, leave aside diagnosing the whole being. The symptoms, therefore, soon reappear. The focus is more on knowing the remedies than on knowing the client. The treatment is rarely sustained beyond a single consultation. Such practitioners may be called remedy-centric practitioners.

Stage Two – Addressing Conditions

This is the stage where the practitioner would study the condition/disease, uncover the cluster of symptoms that the condition displays and combine the remedies in one or two composites and administer over a sustained period of time to address the condition in entirety. The root cause of the condition would remain unknown and unaddressed. Healing therefore would be temporary. More often than not there would be some one-size-fits all solutions for certain conditions which the practitioner would prescribe and administer. Such practitioners may be called solution-centric practitioners.

Stage Three – Healing & Transforming lives

This today is the most advanced stage of evolution. The practitioner is inclined and equipped to know the client at a reasonable level of depth, often to the very root of the client's being. He prefers to have a complete emotional landscape of the client right at the beginning of the treatment and creates a sort of treatment plan. He is more focused on healing the individual than the illness and stays committed to accompany the client on her healing journey, which could take anywhere between 6 months to a year or even more. The goal of the practitioner here is to heal the client, completely and comprehensively and in the process of the healing lead the client to transform. Such practitioners may be called client-centric practitioners.

This third stage of evolution has been pioneered by yours truly and my institution - *All That Bach*. Here the focus is in helping the client to transform her life using Bach Flower essences. This phenomenon completely re-defines and enhances the scope of and expectation from this modality. It's not a new thing: you just need to see the process with new eyes. The root of the word 'heal', 'health', 'holy' and 'whole' is the same. As an individual begins to heal, the shadows start dissolving, making her more 'holy'. Eventually, with the journey being sustained, the individual returns back to being an integrated 'whole' being - from a fragmented mind-made sense of what she is. She goes through a process of complete transformation reclaiming the glory of who she truly is.

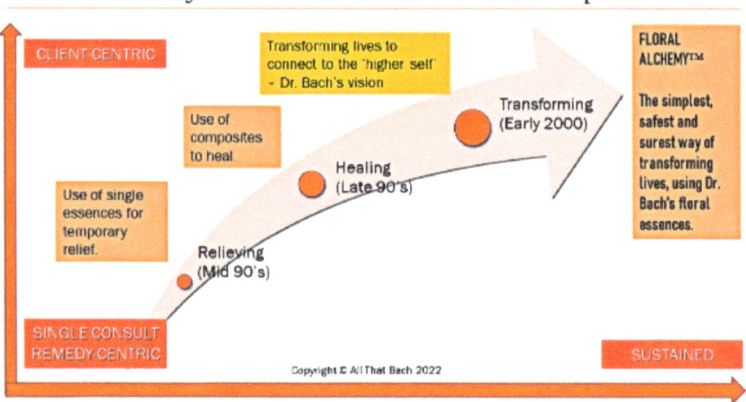

This alchemical journey is beautifully expressed by Dr. Edward Bach, as follows:

"Suffering is a corrective to point out a lesson which by other means we have failed to grasp, and never can it be eradicated until that lesson is learnt. Humans have a soul which is their real higher self; a Divine, Mighty, Being."

I have consciously chosen to therefore re-christen this process of transitioning to a realm of light and virtues with the help of Dr. Bach's 'remedies' as Floral Alchemy™. While on the one-hand this expands the scope and application of the enabling and healing process, on the other it takes away the connotation of illness and something being amiss associated with the word like 'therapy' and 'remedy'. After all, going by Dr. Bach's quote above, 'suffering' is just a state of being without any negative or diminishing connotation. It's just a wake-up alarm.

Floral Alchemy™ is the safest, simplest and surest way of transforming lives of individuals to reclaim the whole being, catalysed by the 38 floral essences that are purely vibrational, without any chemicals, gentle, safe and without any side effect. It is the future of Bach Flower practice.

What emanates from your authentic silence is far more impactful than packaged speech.
Be authentic.
Be silent.

- Indroneil

CHAPTER 5
Physical Ailments & Recommended Bach Flower Essences

Dr. Edward Bach chose not to focus on physical ailments probably because he believed they could distract from understanding the emotional causes of disease. People often talk only about their physical symptoms and overlook the need to heal underlying negative beliefs. Since illness starts in the mind, Dr. Bach aimed to address these root causes to help relieve and heal physical problems.

This doesn't mean physical ailments are ignored; they can definitely be treated. This book explains Dr. Bach's approach, connecting symptoms to emotions and essences while highlighting the importance of emotional healing. The list provided below serves as a helpful reference, showing that healing of physical ailments can happen alongside restoring emotional well-being. It emphasises the need to still consider emotions during the consultation and diagnosis, highlighting that true healing involves both the mind and the body.

In this context, I've compiled a list of physical conditions along with their probable emotional causes. Additionally, I have identified the corresponding rRecommended Bach Flower Essences that can help alleviate these emotional imbalances, ultimately offering relief and healing for the associated physical ailments.

Physical Ailment	Probable Emotional Cause	Recommended Bach Flower Essences
A		
Abdominal Cramps	Women sometimes fear embodying feminine characteristics which can be a barrier to growth and lead to rejecting those qualities. Men's fears, in this context, are often different.	Mimulus, Rock Rose, Cherry Plum. Chicory for fear of being feminine Crab Apple for the cleansing of the endometrium, Walnut to aid in the process of renewal Honeysuckle for letting go off the old
Abscess	Nursing grudges and cultivating thoughts of vengeance.	Holly, Willow, Pine, White Chestnut, Walnut, Star of Bethlehem
Accidents	The inability to advocate for oneself, a rebellious attitude toward authority, and a belief in the use of force.	Centaury, Vine, Vervain
Aches	A deep desire for affection and physical closeness.	Honeysuckle, Chicory, Willow, White Chestnut, Walnut
Acne	Self-rejection and self loathing	Crab Apple Holly if they are red and / or hot

70

Physical Ailment	Probable Emotional Cause	Recommended Bach Flower Essences
Addictions	A fear of introspection and self-confrontation, coupled with a lack of self-live. This can manifest as addictive or compulsive behaviours, driven by a feeling of inadequacy or emptiness.	Agrimony, Crab Apple, Chestnut Bud, Chicory (binge) Cherry Plum
Addisons's Disease	Profound emotional neglect, leading to self-directed anger.	Agrimony, Pine
Adenoids	Discord within the family, leading the child to feel unwanted or a burden.	Holly, Willow, Vine
Adrenal Problems	A sense of hopelessness and resignation, leading to self-neglect and accompanied by anxiety.	Gentian, Wild Rose, Crab Apple, Aspen, Cherry Plum, White Chestnut, Walnut
Aging Problems	Outdated societal norms and ingrained thought patterns create a fear of authenticity and a rejection of the present moment.	Honeysuckle, Agrimony
AIDS	A sense of vulnerability and despair, coupled with the belief that one is unworthy of care and live. This can lead to self-denial and feeling of shame related to sexuality.	Centaury, Gorse, Chicory, Crab Apple, Pine

71

Physical Ailment	Probable Emotional Cause	Recommended Bach Flower Essences
Alcoholism	A pervasive sense of worthlessness, guilt and failure, leading to self-hatred, avoidance, and a lack of motivation, often manifesting in habitual behaviours.	Wild Rose Pine, Crab Apple, Agrimony Cherry Plum Chestnut Bud, Walnut
Allergy	A feeling of disempowerment, lack of control, and an inability to accept oneself or others.	Centaury, Cherry Plum Beech
Alzheimer's Disease	A rejection of reality, coupled with feelings of despair, powerlessness, and anger, along with a sense of being out of control. Lack of control.	Clematis, White Chestnut, Gorse Sweet Chestnut, Holly, Cherry Plum
Amenorrhea	A rejection of one's female identity and a dislike of oneself.	Chicory, Willow Crab Apple
Amnesia	A sense of fear and avoidance of life's challenges, coupled with an inability to assert oneself.	Mimulus, Agrimony, Centaury
Anemia	A perpetually negative outlook, an inability to experience joy, a fear of living fully, and a persistent feeling if inadequacy.	Gentian, Wild Rose, Mimulus, Crab Apple,

Physical Ailment	Probable Emotional Cause	Recommended Bach Flower Essences
Anorectal Bleeding (Hematochezia)	Resentment and exasperation.	Holly, Willow
Anorexia	State of profound self-negation, marked by intense fear, self-hatred, and a feeling of being rejected.	Rock Water Rock Rose, Mimulus Crab Apple, Pine
Annus Abscess	This refers to the anger associated with an unwillingness to relinquish something.	Agrimony, Holly
Annus Fistula	Not fully processing and letting go of past experiences or emotional baggage.	Agrimony, Crab Apple
Annus Itching (Pruritis Ani)	Regret and a sense of responsibility for past actions or omissions.	Pine, Honeysuckle
Annus Pain	A complex of feelings including guilt, a possible desire for punitive consequences, and a sense of inadequacy.	Pine, Crab Apple

Physical Ailment	Probable Emotional Cause	Recommended Bach Flower Essences
Anxiety	Lack of faith in the natural unfolding of events and the inherent rhythm of life.	Gentian, Aspen, Cherry Plum, White Chestnut, Walnut, Rock Rose (If required), Agrimony (for material worries)
Apathy	Emotional suppression, characterised by an avoidance of feelings, a sense of detachment or numbness, an underlying fear.	Wild Rose
Appendicitis	Apprehension and dread related to life itself, which interferes with the ability to experience positive things.	Mimulus, Rock Water
Appetite, Excessive	Fear coupled with a desire for safety, and a tendency to critically evaluate or suppress one's own emotions.	Mimulus, Chicory, Pine
Appetite loss	Fear based need for self preservation, where the individual attempts to create a barrier against perceived dangers from the external environment.	Mimulus

Physical Ailment	Probable Emotional Cause	Recommended Bach Flower Essences
Arteriosclerosis	Rigidity and inflexibility, both physically and mentally characterised by resistance to change, a constricted perspective, and an inability to recognise positive aspects.	Impatiens, Rock Water, Willow, Beech
Arthritic Fingers	A desire for retribution, inflexibility, assigning blame and a sense of being wronged	Vine, Rock Water, Willow, Willow
Arthritis	Feeling lack of affection, coupled with critical judgement and lingering bitterness.	Chicory, Beech, Willow
Asphyxiating Attacks	State of fear, a lack of faith in life's natural progression, and a tendency to regress to or remain fixated on childhood experiences or patterns.	Gentian, Aspen, Walnut
Arthritis (Rheumatoid)	Perceiving oneself as a constant victim, accompanied by persistent negativity, resentment, and a dense of not being loved.	Willow, Chicory
Asthma	Overwhelmed by excess affection, resulting in a sense of suffocation, inability to express oneself freely, and suppressed emotions.	Chicory, Elm, Agrimony

Physical Ailment	Probable Emotional Cause	Recommended Bach Flower Essences
Athlete's Foot	Frustration stemming from a lack of acceptance, coupled with difficulty in progressing smoothly.	Willow, Rock Water
B		
Back Problems		
Lower Back Pain	Fear related to financial resources, specifically the fear of not having enough money or lacking adequate financial support. .	Aspen, Agrimony
Mid-Back Pain	Feeling of guilt and being trapped by past experiences, coupled with defensive reaction and a desire to be left alone.	Pine, Honeysuckle, Willow
Upper Back Pain	Perceived absence of emotional support, a feeling of being unloved, and a tendency to withhold affection.	Chicory, Willow, Agrimony
Back Curvature	Resistance to life's natural flow and support, driven by fear, attachment to outdated beliefs, distrust in life's process, a lack of internal moral compass, and a lack of bravery to stand by one's beliefs.	Rock Water, Aspen, Mimulus, Honeysuckle, Gentian. Agrimony, Larch

Physical Ailment	Probable Emotional Cause	Recommended Bach Flower Essences
Bad Breath	Resentment and vengeful thoughts. Past experiences piling up. Reliving the trauma to validate a point. A need to say, 'I was right.')	Holly, Willow, Star of Beth. Honeysuckle, White Chestnut, Walnut
Balance, Loss of	Vacillating mind. Lacking balance.	Scleranthus
Baldness	Fear and anxiety. Pressure. The urge to manage everything.	Impatiens, Cherry Plum, White Chestnut, Aspen, Walnut
Bedwetting	Apprehension toward a parent, often the father.	Mimulus, Centaury,/Larch, Cherry plum
Belching	Anxiety. Rushing through life too fast.	Mimulus, Impatiens
Bell's Palsy	Rigid suppression of anger. Resistance to expressing emotions.	Rock Water, Agrimony , Holly
Bites	Sensitive to every criticism. Fear.	Mimulus, Centaury
Bites Animal	Repressed self-directed anger. A desire for self-punishment.	Pine

Physical Ailment	Probable Emotional Cause	Recommended Bach Flower Essences
Blackheads	Brief and sudden flashes of anger and irritation.	Holly, Cherry Plum
Bladder Problems	Nervous tension. Clinging to outdated beliefs. Fear of release. Inner frustration.	Aspen, Rock Water, Honeysuckle, Agrimony, Willow
Retention of Urine		
Excessive Urination	Mind and body not in control.	Cherry Plum
Bleeding	Drained happiness. Rising anger.	Cherry Plum, Holly, Mustard
Bleeding Gums	Discontent with life choices. Absence of joy in decisions made.	Willow, Mustard
Blisters	Struggle against change. Vulnerability to emotional harm.	Chicory, Willow, Walnut Agrimony, Impatiens Vine (Resistance to Authority)
Blood Pressure	Longstanding emotional problem not solved.	Vervain, Cherry Plum, Scleranthus
High		

Physical Ailment	Probable Emotional Cause	Recommended Bach Flower Essences
Blood Pressure		Chicory, Willow
Low	Lack of love as a child. Defeatism.	As per experience this works in some cases too: -Hornbeam, Larch, Cherry Plum, Wild Rose Emergency Low BP – Wild Rose, Hornbeam, Rescue Remedy
Blood Problems	Blocking the experience of joy. Self-denial.	Rock Water
Clotting		
Body Odour	Self-rejection. Apprehension and fear toward others.	Crab Apple, Mimulus, Aspen
Bones fracture	Defiance against control.	Holly, Vine
Bowels Problems	Anxiety about releasing the past and things no longer necessary.	Honeysuckle, Agrimony, Crab Apple
Brain tumour	Faulty, rigid beliefs. Stubbornness. Reluctance to change old habits.	Rock Water, Vine, Honeysuckle Walnut

Physical Ailment	Probable Emotional Cause	Recommended Bach Flower Essences
Breast cysts	Neglecting self-care. Prioritising others. Overbearing nurturing. Excessive protection. Dominating others.	Centaury, Chicory, Red Chestnut, Crab apple
Breathing problem	Symbolises the capacity to embrace life. Distrust in life's journey. Stagnation in past experiences. Fear of fully engaging with life.	Mimulus, Larch, Aspen, Gentian, Honeysuckle, Walnut.
Brights's Disease *See Nephritis*	Feeling like a child unable to succeed, inadequate, or a failure. A sense of loss.	Larch, Crab Apple
Bronchitis	Tense family atmosphere. Conflict and arguments.	Willow, Vine, White Chestnut Walnut
Bruises	Minor challenges in life. Self-inflicted punishment.	Pine
Bulimia	Overwhelming fear, feeling hopeless. A desperate cycle of intake and release of self-loathing.	Rock Rose, Gorse, Scleranthus, Impatiens, Cherry Plum, Crab Apple
Bunions	Absence of joy in facing life's experiences.	Wild Rose

Physical Ailment	Probable Emotional Cause	Recommended Bach Flower Essences
Burns	Fury. Seething. Enraged.	Holly, Cherry Plum, White Chestnut, Walnut, Star of Bethlehem
Bursitis	Suppressed rage. A desire to lash out.	Holly, Vine, White Chestnut, Walnut
C		
Callouses	Rigid beliefs and ideas. Fear entrenched.	Rock Water, Mimulus, White Chestnut, Aspen, Walnut.
Cancer	Profound pain. Lasting bitterness. A hidden sorrow or grief gnawing at the self, harbouring hatred.	Star of Bethlehem, Honeysuckle, Willow, Agrimony. Sweet Chestnut, Holly
Candida	Feeling unfocused and overwhelmed. Deep frustration and anger. Demanding and distrustful in relationships. Tendency to take more than give.	Scleranthus, Willow, Holly, Chicory, Elm
Canker Sores	Unspoken, lingering words. Suppressed blame.	Holly, Willow, White Chestnut, Walnut
Carpal Tunnel Syndrome	Resentment and frustration over life's perceived unfairness.	Holly, Willow, Vervain

Physical Ailment	Probable Emotional Cause	Recommended Bach Flower Essences
Cataracts	Difficulty envisioning a joyful future. A sense of darkness ahead.	Wild Rose, Gentian, Mustard
Cellulite	Repressed rage and self-inflicted suffering.	Holly, Willow, Pine, White Chestnut, Walnut
Cerebral Palsy	A desire to bring the family together through love and unity.	Chicory, Scleranthus, Rock Rose, Cherry Plum, WCN (Covers symptoms also)
Chills	Mind closing in, withdrawing inward. Longing to retreat.	Hornbeam, Mustard, Mimulus
Cholesterol	Blocking the flow of joy. Fear of embracing happiness.	Gentian, Rock Water, Aspen
Chronic Disease	Resistance to change. Anxiety about the future. Lack of security.	Mimulus, Aspen, Walnut
Colds	Overwhelmed by chaos. Mental fog and disarray. Lingering minor wounds.	Scleranthus, Hornbeam, Willow, White Chestnut, Walnut
Colic	Insecurity. Represents the ease of letting go of that which is over.	Honeysuckle, Agrimony

Physical Ailment	Probable Emotional Cause	Recommended Bach Flower Essences
Colon	Can't let go of the past out of fear.	Honeysuckle, White Chestnut, Walnut, Aspen
Coma	Fear. Running away from something or someone out of fear.	Mimulus, Clematis, Aspen
Comedones (clogged pores)	Occasional mild outbursts of anger.	Holly, Cherry Plum
Conjunctivitis	A view of life causing anger and frustration.	Holly, Willow, Beech, Cherry Plum, White Chestnut, Walnut
Constipation	Retention of what must go away, including guilt, from the past, leading to incomplete evacuation. Sometimes could be unwillingness to spend money.	Agrimony, Honeysuckle, Pine, Chicory
Corns	Not letting go of past pains and traumas, made to persist with stubborn and unchanging thoughts.	Rock Water, Vine, Honeysuckle, White Chestnut, Star of Bethlehem, Walnut
Coughs	Feeling unheard, 'barking' to seek audience and attention.	Vervain, Heather, Cherry Plum

Physical Ailment	Probable Emotional Cause	Recommended Bach Flower Essences
Cramps	Gripping fear causing anxiety. Holding on.	Agrimony, Mimulus, Rock Rose, Aspen
Crohn's Disease	Anxiety and fear. Low self-esteem.	Mimulus, Aspen, White Chestnut, Walnut, Crab Apple
Crying	Spontaneous flow of intense joy, sadness and fear.	Cherry Plum
Cuts	Self-righteous and self-punishing for not abiding by ones' own principles.	Rock Water, Pine
Cysts	Repeated recall of old traumas and pain, keeping alive hurts of the past. Pretension of having moved on and grown.	Honeysuckle, Willow, Chicory, Agrimony
Cystic Fibrosis	Firm pessimism about life not going to work out, leading to self-pity.	Willow, Gentian
D		
Deafness	Avoidance, resistance, solitude. What words do you dread? "Leave me alone."	Water Violet, Vine, Beech
Diabetes	Yearning for lost possibilities. An overwhelming desire for control. Profound grief. All warmth has faded.	Honeysuckle, Impatience, Sweet Chestnut, Gorse, Willow

Physical Ailment	Probable Emotional Cause	Recommended Bach Flower Essences
Diarrhea	Dread. Abandonment. Fleeing.	Aspen, Impatiens, Beech, Cherry Plum, Crab Apple, SOB
Dizziness	Restless, unfocused mind. An unwillingness to see.	Scleranthus, Agrimony / Water Violet
Dry eyes	Fierce glare. Rejecting love's perspective. Choosing resentment over forgiveness. Clinging to spite.	Holly, Willow, Vine Dry eyes denote dryness of tears – Sweet Chestnut.
Dysentery - Amoebic, Bacillary	Terror and raging fury.	Mimulus, Holly, Vine
Dysmenorrhea	Self-directed rage. Contempt for the body or resentment toward women.	Pine, Crab Apple, Chicory
E		
Earache	Frustration, refusal to listen, overwhelming chaos, conflict between parents.	Water Violet, Willow, Holly
Eczema	Stunning hostility. Explosive thoughts.	Holly, Vine, Cherry Plum, Crab Apple
Edema	What or who are you still holding onto?	Honeysuckle, Agrimony, Walnut

Physical Ailment	Probable Emotional Cause	Recommended Bach Flower Essences
Emphysema	Fear of embracing life. Feeling unworthy of living.	Mimulus, Larch, Crab Apple
Endometriosis	Self-doubt, disillusionment, and frustration. Substituting self-care with sweets. Accusers.	Larch, Aspen, Gentian, Chicory, Willow
Epilepsy	Constant fear of being persecuted. Rejection of life. A deep sense of inner turmoil. Self-inflicted harm.	Larch, Aspen, WCN, Cherry Plum, Willow, Pine.
Epstein-Barr Virus	Pushing beyond one's limits. Fear of not being good enough. Draining all inner support. Stress.	Elm, Larch, Crab Apple, Olive, Oak
Eye problems	Fear of seeing the self	Agrimony
Astigmatism		
Hyperopia	Fear of the present.	Mimulus, Clematis
Myopia	Fear of the future.	Aspen
F		
Fainting	Terror. Overwhelmed. Fading into darkness.	Clematis

Physical Ailment	Probable Emotional Cause	Recommended Bach Flower Essences
Fat or Weight issues	Heightened sensitivity. Often stems from fear and a desire for protection. Fear may mask hidden anger and resistance to forgiveness. Avoiding emotions. Insecurity, self-rejection, and searching for fulfilment.	Mimulus, Aspen, Holly, Willow, Agrimony, Cherry Plum, Crab Apple, Chestnut Bud
	Arms: Anger at being denied love.	Chicory, Willow, Holly
	Belly: Anger at being denied nourishment.	Chicory, Holly
	Hips: Lumps of stubborn anger at the parents.	Vine
	Thighs: Packed childhood anger. Often rage at the father.	Honeysuckle, Holly, Vine
Fatigue	Reluctance, monotony. Absence of passion for one's work.	Wild Rose, Chestnut Bud, Olive, Oak.
Fever	Burning up with anger.	Holly, Rescue Remedy

Physical Ailment	Probable Emotional Cause	Recommended Bach Flower Essences
Fibroid Tumours	Holding onto pain from a partner. A wound to the feminine pride.	Willow, Chicory, Star of Bethlehem
Fistula	Fear - an obstacle to the process of letting go.	Mimulus, Crab Apple, Agrimony
Food Poisoning	Giving control to others and feeling vulnerable.	Centaury, Beech, Crab Apple
Foot Problems	A fear of the unknown and the inability to move forward in life.	Aspen, Larch, Hornbeam
Frigidity	Fear. Rejection of pleasure. The belief that sex is wrong. Unaware or unempathetic partners. Fear of the father.	Rock Water, Crab Apple, Mimulus, Larch Add White Chestnut if the partner is pre-occupied. Add Hornbeam with the partner is fatigued Add Vervain when the partner is very driven towards another cause.
Fungus	Stagnant beliefs. Holding on to the past. Allowing the past to control the present.	Honeysuckle, Rock Water, Crab Apple

Physical Ailment	Probable Emotional Cause	Recommended Bach Flower Essences
G		
Gallstones	Bitterness, harsh judgments, a critical spirit, and an inflated sense of self-importance.	Willow, Beech, Vine, Water Violet
Gangrene	A state of mental gloom, where toxic thoughts suffocate and overwhelm any sense of joy.	Mustard, Willow, Cherry Plum, White Chestnut, Walnut.
Gas	A sense of being trapped, consumed by fear, and burdened by thoughts that remain unresolved or unprocessed.	Rock Rose, Mimulus, Beech
Gastritis	Ongoing uncertainty. A sense of impending doom.	White Chestnut, Walnut, Aspen, Gentian, Gorse
Glandular Problems	Ineffective distribution of motivation and ideas. Holding yourself back.	Hornbeam
Glaucoma	Unyielding unforgiveness. The weight of deep, lingering wounds. Feeling overwhelmed by it all.	Willow, Honeysuckle, Elm, SOB
Gout	The desire to control. Impatience and anger.	Vine, Impatiens, Holly

Physical Ailment	Probable Emotional Cause	Recommended Bach Flower Essences
Gray Hair	Stress. The belief in constant pressure and strain.	Oak, Impatiens, White Chestnut, Walnut
Growths	Focusing on old wounds. Holding onto resentments.	Honeysuckle, Willow, White Chestnut, Walnut, SOB
Gum Problems	Inability to stand by decisions. Uncertainty about life.	Cerato, Wild Oat, Larch
H		
Hay Fever	Emotional blockage. Anxiety about time passing. Perceived victimisation. Feelings of guilt.	Agrimony, Aspen, Larch, Willow, Pine
Headaches	Undermining oneself. Self-criticism. Fear.	Pine, Crab Apple, Larch
Heart problems	Neglecting personal happiness in pursuit of financial gain or status, leading to feelings of isolation and fear. Internalizing thoughts such as, "I'm inadequate. I don't accomplish enough. Success is unattainable."	Heart Attack Agrimony, Chicory, Mimulus, Heather, Crab Apple, Pine, Larch, Gentian

Physical Ailment	Probable Emotional Cause	Recommended Bach Flower Essences
Heart problems	Persistent emotional distress and a lack of joy can lead to a metaphorical hardening of the heart, contributing to cardiovascular issues. The belief in constant pressure and stress further exacerbates these problems. Chronic stress has been linked to increased risk factors for heart disease, including high blood pressure and inflammation	Honeysuckle, Willow, Mustard, Holly, Impatiens, Oak
Heartburn	Fear. Fear. Fear. Gripping fear..	Rock Rose, Mimulus, Aspen,
Hemorrhoids	Experiencing anxiety about upcoming deadlines, harboring resentment over past events, fearing the act of letting go, and feeling overwhelmed by burdens are interconnected emotional challenges. Anxiety about deadlines can lead to procrastination and increased stress, while unresolved anger from past experiences may contribute to ongoing emotional distress. The fear of releasing control or moving on can exacerbate feelings of being overwhelmed.	Hornbeam, Mimulus, Honeysuckle, Holly, White Chestnut, Walnut, Oak

Physical Ailment	Probable Emotional Cause	Recommended Bach Flower Essences
Hepatitis	Resistance to change often stems from emotions such as fear, anger, and hatred. In traditional Chinese medicine, the liver is associated with anger and rage.	Aspen, Mimulus, Holly, Willow, Vine
Hernia	Broken relationships. Tension, heavy burdens, and misdirected creative expression.	Willow, Oak, Elm, Clematis, Agrimony
Herpes Genitalis	Widespread belief in sexual guilt and the need for retribution. Public humiliation. Perception of a punitive God. Rejection of one's own sexuality.	Pine, Crab Apple, Willow
Herpes Simplex	Unspoken words filled with bitterness.	Willow, Centaury/Agrimony / Water Violet
Hip problems	The fear of moving forward with major decisions, with no clear direction or purpose to pursue.	Scleranthus, Larch, Wild Rose
Hirsutism	Anger that is suppressed, often masked by fear. A tendency to assign blame, coupled with a frequent reluctance to care for oneself.	Agrimony, Holly, Willow, Aspen

Physical Ailment	Probable Emotional Cause	Recommended Bach Flower Essences
Hives	Minor, concealed fears that are blown out of proportion, turning small issues into overwhelming obstacles.	Agrimony, Heather, Holly, Crab Apple
Hodgkin's Disease	A deep-seated fear of inadequacy and a tendency to blame oneself or others. This drives a relentless, exhausting pursuit to prove one's worth, draining all vitality until there's nothing left to sustain oneself. In this desperate quest for validation, the simple joy of living is lost	Willow, Crab Apple, Impatiens, Oak, Wild Rose
Huntington's Disease	Frustration and bitterness from the inability to change others, leading to a sense of hopelessness.	Vine, Gorse
Hyperactivity	Fear, coupled with a sense of being overwhelmed and rushed, creating a frantic state of mind.	Elm, Impatiens, Aspen
Hyperventilation	Fear of embracing change and a lack of trust in the natural flow of life.	Mimulus, Impatiens

Physical Ailment	Probable Emotional Cause	Recommended Bach Flower Essences
Hypoglycemia	Feeling weighed down and consumed by the heavy responsibilities and challenges of life	Oak, Elm
Heitis (Crohn's Disease, Regional Enteritis)	Fear and anxiety, rooted in a persistent sense of inadequacy and self-doubt..	Aspen, Cherry Plum, White Chestnut, Crab Apple, Walnut
I		
Impotence	Emotional turmoil stemming from sexual pressure, tension, and guilt, influenced by societal expectations. Resentment toward a past partner and an underlying fear of one's mother further complicate these feelings.	Elm, Larch, Pine, Rock water, Holly, Honeysuckle, Walnut, Mimulus
Incontinence	A buildup of suppressed emotions over the years, leading to an overwhelming and uncontrollable emotional release	Cherry Plum, Agrimony, Walnut
Indigestion	Intense, instinctual fear, deep-seated dread, and persistent anxiety, often accompanied by complaints and expressions of frustration.	Aspen, Mimulus, Rockrose, Willow, Beech

Physical Ailment	Probable Emotional Cause	Recommended Bach Flower Essences
Infection	Feelings of irritation, anger, and frustration, often stemming from a sense of being tainted or contaminated by external influences.	Holly, Beech, Willow, Impatiens Crab Apple
Inflammation	Fear and intense anger, leading to heated, irrational thoughts and overwhelming frustration.	Mimulus, Willow, Holly, White chestnut
Influenza	A reaction to widespread negativity and collective beliefs, driven by fear and an over-reliance on statistical probabilities.	Centaury, Gentian, Cerato, Mimulus
Ingrown Toenail	Anxiety and self-doubt about whether you deserve to progress or take the next step in life.	Centaury, WCN, Pine, Larch
Injuries	Self-directed anger and a deep sense of guilt.	Pine
Insanity	Avoiding family responsibilities, seeking escape, withdrawing emotionally, and harboring intense, aggressive thoughts.	Clematis, Wild Rose, Cherry Plum, Vine

Physical Ailment	Probable Emotional Cause	Recommended Bach Flower Essences
Insomnia	Fear and a lack of trust in the natural flow of life, often accompanied by feelings of guilt.	Aspen, Pine, Impatiens, White Chestnut, Walnut
Itching	Cravings that defy the norm, leaving one restless and regretful.	Agrimony, Crabapple, Beech, Cherry plum, WCN, Aspen, Walnut
J		
Jaundice	Biases both within oneself and from others. Skewed judgment.	Beech, Cherry plum, Scleranthus, Crab Apple
Jaw Problems	Fury, bitterness, and a thirst for retaliation.	Holly, Willow
K		
Kidney Problems	Judgment, letdown, setbacks. Humiliation. Reacting	Beech, Gentian, Larch, Pine, Crab apple
Kidney Stones	Pockets of unresolved fury.	Holly, Rock Water, Crab Apple
Knee problem	Unyielding self-importance and arrogance.	Vine, Rock water
L		
Laryngitis	Speechless with rage. Intimidated to voice opinions. Hostility towards power.	Centaury, Holly, Willow, Rock Rose

Physical Ailment	Probable Emotional Cause	Recommended Bach Flower Essences
Leg problems	Apprehension about what's to come. Reluctance to take action.	Larch, Hornbeam, Aspen
Leprosy	Incapacity to cope with life's demands. Persistent feeling of inadequacy or unworthiness.	Larch, Crab Apple, Pine, White Chestnut Walnut
Liver	Root of rage and primal feelings. Habitual grumbling. Rationalizing criticism to self-deceive. Feeling down.	Holly, Vervain, Willow, Vine
Lockjaw	Rage, a need for dominance, and a reluctance to reveal emotions.	Holly, Vine
Lump in the Throat	Anxiety and skepticism towards life's journey.	Aspen, Impatiens
Lung problems	Capacity to embrace life. Melancholy. Sorrow. Sense of unworthiness to experience life fully.	SOB, Wild Rose, Sweet Chestnut, Crab Apple, Mustard. Gorse
Lupus	A sense of surrender. Belief that it's preferable to give up rather than defend oneself. Deep-seated rage and a penchant for self-punishment.	Pine, Wild Rose, Holly
Lymph Problems	A reminder that the mind must refocus on life's core values—love and joy.	Wild Oat, Wild Rose, Scleranthus, Holly

Physical Ailment	Probable Emotional Cause	Recommended Bach Flower Essences
M		
Malaria	Disconnected from the harmony of nature and the rhythms of life	Scleranthus, Wild Rose, Crab Apple
Mastoiditis	Rage and irritation. A wish to block out the surrounding noise. Often observed in children. Anxiety clouding comprehension.	Holly, Willow, Aspen
Menopause Problems	Dread of abandonment and aging. Self-denial. Feelings of inadequacy.	Crab Apple, Pine, Walnut, Chicory, Honeysuckle, Aspen
Menstrual Problems	Denial of one's feminine qualities. Feelings of guilt and fear. Perception that one's genitals are shameful or impure.	Chicory, Pine, Crab Apple, Aspen
Migraine Headaches	Aversion to being controlled. Opposition to life's natural course. Anxieties related to sexuality.	Vine, Rock water, Mimulus, Crab Apple
Miscarriage	Apprehension about what's ahead. Misjudged timing.	Aspen, Impatiens, Willow

Physical Ailment	Probable Emotional Cause	Recommended Bach Flower Essences
Miscarriage	Fear of the future. Inappropriate timing.	Aspen, Impatiens, Willow
Mononucleosis - Fatigue, Sore throat, perhaps misdiagnosed as strep throat, that doesn't get better after treatment with antibiotics, Fever Swollen lymph nodes in your neck and armpits, Swollen tonsils, Headache, Skin rash, Soft, swollen spleen	Resentment due to lack of love and recognition. Neglect of self-care..	Chicory, Centaury, Rescue Remedy, Crab Apple
Motion Sickness	Anxiety, restriction, and a sense of entrapment..	Mimulus, Scleranthus,
Multiple Sclerosis	Rigidity of mind, lack of compassion, unyielding determination, and stubbornness.	Rock water, Holly, Vine
Muscular Dystrophy	Feeling that maturing is not worthwhile.	Gentian, Chicory
N		
Nail Biting	Exasperation. Self-eroding resentment. Animus toward a parent.	Willow

Physical Ailment	Probable Emotional Cause	Recommended Bach Flower Essences
Narcolepsy	Can't cope. Extreme fear. Wanting to get away from it all. Not wanting to be here.	Elm, Rock Rose, Aspen, Clematis
Nausea	Anxiety. Resisting the acceptance of a concept or situation.	Mimulus, Aspen, Willow, Beech
Neck stiffness	Stubbornness. Blindness to the past. Unwillingness to consider alternative perspectives.	Rock water, Vine, Vervain
Nephritis	Intense reaction to setbacks and perceived failures.	Gentian, Cherry Plum
Nervous Breakdown	Narcissism, obstructing lines of dialogue.	Heather, Vine
Nervousness	Apprehension, unease, conflict, and haste. Doubt in the natural flow of life.	Mimulus, Aspen, Rock Rose, Cherry Plum, Impatiens
Neuralgia	Penalisation driven by guilt. Distress in conveying messages.	Pine, Sweet Chestnut
Nodules	Bitterness, irritation, and wounded pride related to one's profession.	Willow, SOB
Nose Bleeds	A yearning for acknowledgment. Feelings of invisibility. Desperate plea for affection.	Chicory

Physical Ailment	Probable Emotional Cause	Recommended Bach Flower Essences
Nose Runny	Reaching out for assistance. Silent weeping within.	Sweet Chestnut, Chicory
Nose Stuffy	Lack of acknowledgment of one's own value.	Crab Apple, Heather
Numbness	Withholding love and consideration. Going dead mentally.	Holly, Clematis
O		
Osteomyelitis	Rage and exasperation towards the fundamental aspects of existence. A sense of being unassisted.	Holly, Willow, Chicory
Osteoporosis	A sense of abandoned support. Mental strain and rigidity. Inability for muscles to extend. Diminished mental flexibility.	Sweet Chestnut, Elm, Hornbeam
P		
Paget's Disease	A sense of a lost foundation. Belief that "Nobody cares."	Chicory, Wild Rose, Gorse
Pain	Guilt, an emotion that often drives a desire for self-punishment.	Pine, Willow, Impatiens
Palsy	Debilitating thoughts. Feeling immobilised.	White Chestnut, Rock Rose

Physical Ailment	Probable Emotional Cause	Recommended Bach Flower Essences
Paralysis	Intense fear. Panic prompting an urge to flee a situation or person.	Rock Rose, Clematis, White Chestnut, Walnut
Pancreas	Symbolises the joys and pleasures of life.	Willow
Pancreatitis	Rejection. Anger and frustration because life seems to have lost its sweetness.	Chicory, Holly, Willow
Parasites	Surrendering control, allowing others to dominate and rely on you.	Centaury, Walnut
Parkinson's Disease	Apprehension coupled with an overwhelming urge to micromanage every aspect and individual.	Mimulus, Aspen, Vine, Impatiens
Peptic Ulcer	Apprehension. Self-doubt and a deep need for approval.	Crab Apple, Centaury, Mimulus, Aspen
Phlebitis	Rage and exasperation. Attributing the constraints and absence of joy in life to others.	Holly, Willow, Wild Rose
Pimples	Minor fits of rage.	Holly, Cherry Plum
Pituitary Gland	Symbolizes the command hub.	Impatiens, Vine

Physical Ailment	Probable Emotional Cause	Recommended Bach Flower Essences
Plantar Wart	Fury rooted in your core beliefs. Widespread vexation concerning what's to come.	Holly, Willow, Aspen
Pneumonia	Desperation. Exhaustion with life. Emotional scars that remain open and unhealed.	Sweet Chestnut, Wild Rose, SOB
Poison Ivy	Allergy. A sense of vulnerability and exposure to harm.	Beech, Crab Apple, Centaury, Walnut
Polio	Crippling envy. A wish to hinder someone.	Holly, Vine, Chicory, Vine
Post nasal Drip	Silent inner weeping. Tears of innocence. A sense of victimhood.	Chicory, Willow
Premenstrual Syndrome	Permitting chaos to dominate. Yielding control to external forces. Dismissing feminine principles.	Chicory, Scleranthus, Centaury, Walnut
Prostate Problems	Psychological anxieties diminish masculinity. Surrendering. Sexual stress and guilt. Acceptance of aging.	Agrimony, Larch, Pine, Crab Apple, Honeysuckle
Psoriasis	Apprehension about being harmed. Numbing one's own senses. Avoiding accountability for personal emotions.	Mimulus, Aspen, Agrimony Pine, Sweet Chestnut

Physical Ailment	Probable Emotional Cause	Recommended Bach Flower Essences
Pyorrhoea (Periodontitis)	Frustration with indecisiveness. Annoyance with fickle individuals.	Cerrato, Scleranthus, Holly, Pine
Q		
Quinsy (Peritonsillar Abscess) Tonsillitis	A deep-seated conviction of being unable to advocate for oneself and express one's needs.	Centaury
R		
Rabies	Fury accompanied by the conviction that violence is a solution.	Holly, Vine
Rash	Frustration with delays. Childish tactics to seek attention.	Impatiens, Heather
Rheumatism	A sense of victimisation. Absence of affection. Persistent bitterness. Deep-seated resentment.	Willow, Chicory
Rheumatoid Arthritis	Profound disapproval of authority. A strong sense of being burdened.	Beech, Centaury
Rickets	Emotional malnutrition. Lack of love and security.	Chicory, Agrimony

Physical Ailment	Probable Emotional Cause	Recommended Bach Flower Essences
Ringworm	Letting others irritate you. Struggling with self-worth or feeling unclean.	Century, Crab Apple
Round Shoulders (See Shoulders, Spinal Curvature)	Bearing the weight of life's challenges. Feeling powerless and despairing.	Oak, Sweet Chestnut, Gorse
S		
Sagging Lines	Drooping facial lines mirror drooping thoughts. Bitterness towards life.	Gentian, Gorse, White Chestnut, Walnut
Scabies	Contaminated mindset. Permitting others to irritate you.	Centaury, Crabapple, White Chestnut, Walnut
Sciatica	Displaying double standards. Anxiety about finances and the uncertainty of the future..	Aspen, Agrimony
Scleroderma	Shielding oneself from life's challenges. Doubting one's ability to provide self-care and support.	Mimulus, Larch, Aspen
Scratches	Feeling like life is tearing you apart. A sense of being cheated by life.	Willow, Beech, White chestnut

Physical Ailment	Probable Emotional Cause	Recommended Bach Flower Essences
Seizures	Fleeing from family, oneself, or life's challenges.	Clematis, Agrimony
Senility	Seeking refuge in the perceived safety of childhood. Craving care and attention. Manipulating others for control. Escapism.	Honeysuckle, Chicory, White Chestnut, Walnut Chicory, Willow, Heather
Shingles	Anticipating disaster. Anxiety and stress. Hyper-sensitivity.	Aspen, Gentian, Mimulus
Sickle Cell Anemia	A conviction of inadequacy, eroding the essence of life's joy.	Crab Apple, Wild Rose
Sinus Problems	Annoyance directed at someone close.	Beech, Impatiens, Holly, Willow, Crab apple, Olive, Cherry Plum
Skin problems	Safeguarding one's individuality. Feelings of anxiety and fear. Repressed, unresolved issues. A sense of being threatened.	Crab apple, Mimulus, Larch, Aspen, Rockrose. Honeysuckle, Willow, White Chestnut, Walnut
Slipped Disc	Experiencing a complete lack of support from life. Struggling with indecisiveness.	Chicory, Cerrato, Scleranthus
Snoring	Persistent resistance to changing old habits..	Vine, Chestnut Bud, White Chestnut, Walnut

Physical Ailment	Probable Emotional Cause	Recommended Bach Flower Essences
Sores	Repressed anger that lingers within.	Holly, Willow, Beech, White chestnut, Walnut
Spasms	Constricting our thoughts due to fear.	Mimulus, Cherry Plum, White Chestnut, Aspen, Walnut
Spinal Curvature (Scoliosis Kyphosis) *See Round Shoulders, Spinal Misalignments*	Inability to align with the natural support of life. Clinging to outdated beliefs out of fear. Distrust in life's processes. Absence of integrity. Lack of commitment to one's principles.	Rock Water Honeysuckle, Aspen, White Chestnut, Walnut Gentian, Agrimony
Spinal Meningitis	Inflamed thoughts and intense anger towards life.	Holly, Pine
Spleen	Fixations. Preoccupied with certain things..	Crab Apple, Cherry Plum
Sprains	Defiance and reluctance. Avoiding a particular path in life.	Holly, Vine
Sterility	Fear and resistance to life's natural progression. Reluctance to experience or participate in parenting..	Chicory, Mimulus, Vine, Walnut

Physical Ailment	Probable Emotional Cause	Recommended Bach Flower Essences
Stiffness	Inflexible, unyielding mindset.	Rock water, Vine, White Chestnut, Walnut
Stomach	Apprehension. Anxiety about unfamiliar experiences. Difficulty adapting to change.	Mimulus, Beech
Stroke	Surrendering. Defiance. Prefer death over change. Renouncing life.	Wild Rose, Vine, Rock Water
Stuttering	Feelings of insecurity. Suppressed self-expression. Inability to release emotions through crying.	Mimulus, larch, Agrimony, Cherry plum, White chestnut, Walnut
Sty	Viewing life through a lens of anger. Resentment towards someone.	Holly, Pine
Suicidal thoughts	Perceiving life in a binary manner. Unwillingness to consider alternative perspectives.	Wild Rose, Mustard, Cherry Plum, White chestnut, Walnut
T		
Tapeworm	Deep-seated conviction of victimhood and impurity. Feeling powerless against others' perceived attitudes.	Willow, Crab Apple, Sweet Chestnut

Physical Ailment	Probable Emotional Cause	Recommended Bach Flower Essences
Teeth Problems	Persistent indecisiveness. Difficulty deconstructing ideas for analysis and decision-making. Root canal - Unable to engage with anything. Core beliefs being shattered.. Impacted wisdom teeth - Restricting yourself from developing a solid mental foundation.	Cerato, Scleranthus Gentian, Larch, Gorse Impatiens, White Chestnut, Walnut
Throat Problems	Inability to assert oneself. Repressed anger. Suppressed creativity. Resistance to change. Sore throat - Suppressed anger. Inability to voice one's thoughts.	Centaury, Agrimony, Clematis, Walnut Agrimony, Holly, White Chestnut, Walnut
Thrush	Frustration due to poor decision-making.	Holly, Pine
Thymus gland problems	Feeling persecuted by life. Paranoia that others are plotting against you.	Willow, Larch, Pine, Aspen
Thyroid problems	Hypothyroid - Feeling humiliated. Constantly denied the opportunity to pursue personal desires. Wondering when your chance will come.	Willow, Larch

Physical Ailment	Probable Emotional Cause	Recommended Bach Flower Essences
Thyroid problems	Hyperthyroid - Intense anger due to feelings of exclusion.	Cherry Plum, Holly, Vine, Chicory
Tics, Twitches	Fear accompanied by the sensation of being observed by others.	Agrimony, Vervain, Cherry Plum, Mimulus, Aspen
Tinnitus or Ringing in the Ears	Resistance to listening. Ignoring one's inner voice. Obstinacy.	Water Violet, Vine
Tongue problems	Lack of joy in experiencing life's pleasures.	Wild Rose, Rock Water
Tonsillitis	Anxiety. Suppressed feelings. Inhibited creativity.	Agrimony, Crab Apple
Tuberculosis	Deteriorating due to self-centeredness. Overly possessive. Harbouring malicious thoughts. Seeking revenge.	Chicory, Holly, Willow, Vine
Tumours	Harbouring past wounds and traumas.	Honeysuckle, Pine, SOB, Walnut
U		
Ulcers	Anxiety. Deep-seated belief in personal inadequacy. Inner turmoil gnawing at one's well-being.	Mimulus, Crab Apple, Willow

Physical Ailment	Probable Emotional Cause	Recommended Bach Flower Essences
Urethritis	Intense anger. Feeling enraged. Assigning blame.	Holly, Willow
Urinary infections	Intense frustration, typically directed at the opposite sex or a partner. Assigning blame to others.	Willow, Chicory, Crab Apple Olive

V

Vaginitis	Anger at a mate. Sexual guilt. Punishing the self.	Holly, Pine Willow. Chicory Crab Apple
Varicose Veins	Standing in a situation you hate. Discouragement. Feeling overworked and overburdened.	Oak, Hornbeam, Gentian, Walnut, Elm
Viral Infections	Lack of joy flowing through life. Bitterness	Wild Rose, Rock Water, Willow
Vitiligo	Feeling completely outside of things. Not belonging. Not one of the groups.	Water violet, Mimulus
Vomiting	Violent rejection of ideas. Fear of the new.	Vervain, Mimulus, Scleranthus, Beech Cherry Plum

W

Warts	Subtle manifestations of hatred. Perception of unattractiveness.	Holly, Crab Apple, Willow

Physical Ailment	Probable Emotional Cause	Recommended Bach Flower Essences
Warts	Plantar warts - Deep-seated anger at foundational beliefs. Widespread frustration regarding future prospects.	Pine, Holly
Weakness	Craving for mental respite.	Hornbeam, Olive, Oak, Elm
Wounds See Cuts, Injuries	Self-directed anger and guilt.	
Wrist problems	Limited physical mobility.	Rock Water
Source: Probable Emotional Cause – Heal your Body, Louise Hay		

The author of this book do not dispense medical advise or prescribe the use of any technique as a form of treatment for physical, emotional or medical problems without the advice of a physician, either directly or indirectly. The intent of the author is only to offer information of a general nature in your quest for emotional and spiritual wellbeing.

In the event you use any of the recommendation given above for yourself the author and the publisher assume no responsibility for your actions.

Bach Flower Essences are without any chemicals and safe. As such they do not have adverse interaction with any other mode of treatment and can be had concomitantly.

Destiny is the experience that you go through this moment, every moment. Free will is what you choose to do with the experience.

- Indroneil

CHAPTER 6
A Special Note on Anxiety

Do you ever feel like no matter what you do, worry just won't let go?

It's normal to feel anxious from time to time, but people with anxiety disorders experience frequent, intense, and overwhelming worry or fear about everyday situations. This anxiety often persists beyond a reasonable level, affecting daily life. Anxiety disorders can also lead to sudden episodes of extreme fear or panic, known as panic attacks, where these feelings peak within a short time.

Anxiety lingers without a clear cause, manifesting as constant worry and fear that can be difficult to shake. It often comes with physical symptoms, such as a racing heart and shortness of breath, and can affect your life even when everything seems fine. In summary, stress is a reaction to immediate challenges, while anxiety reflects ongoing fear about future problems.

The effects of anxiety can be restrictive. Anxiety and panic interfere with daily activities, are difficult to control, are out of proportion to the actual danger and can last a long time. One can always avoid places or situations to prevent these feelings, but unless the illness is cured, it lurks deep inside.

Symptoms of anxiety may start during childhood or the teen years, continuing into adulthood. Moreover, it is believed that women are more prone to anxiety than men.

some cases, this can lead to panic (Rock Rose) or even a nervous breakdown.

Anxiety doesn't just affect the mind it can deeply impact the body as well, leading to physical ailments.

Some of the common signs and symptoms of anxiety include:

Excessive Worrying: Persistent and overwhelming worry that dominates daily life.

Nervousness and Restlessness: Feelings of nervous energy, butterflies in the stomach, or physical restlessness.

Increased Heart Rate and Hyperventilation: Anxiety triggers stress hormones like adrenaline, causing a racing heart and shallow breathing, often leading to dizziness.

Sweating and Trembling: Stress can activate sweat glands and cause trembling due to excess energy.

Fatigue and Weakness: Constant worry drains mental and physical energy, resulting in fatigue.

Difficulty Concentrating: Anxiety monopolises thoughts, making it hard to focus on other tasks.

Sleep Problems: Racing thoughts and physical tension disrupt sleep, making it difficult to fall or stay asleep.

Digestive Issues:
Anxiety can upset the digestive system, causing nausea, diarrhea, or IBS. A churning sensation in the stomach is also common.

Headaches and Muscle Tension: Prolonged anxiety causes muscle tension, which can lead to headaches and chronic pain.

Pins and Needles: Sensations of pins and needles, often in the hands or feet, are common during anxiety episodes.

Sense of Impending Doom: Anxiety can cause the mind to focus on potential threats, heightening emotional responses and reinforcing panic through physiological changes like sweating and increased heart rate.

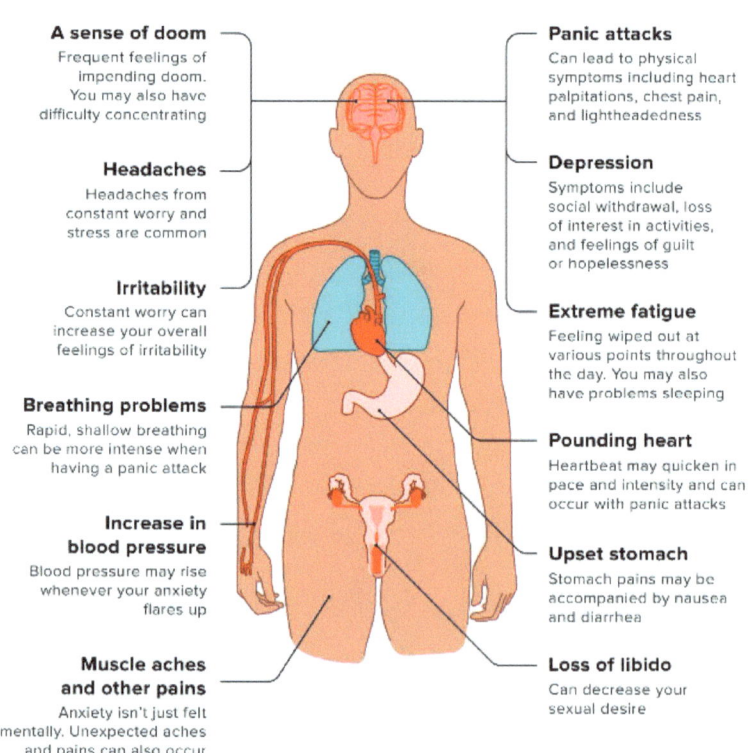

Anxiety comes in many forms, each affecting people in different ways. Some individuals feel intense fear in specific situations, while others deal with a constant sense of dread.

Types of anxiety disorders

Here are some common types of anxiety disorders:

Generalised Anxiety Disorder
Generalised Anxiety Disorder (GAD) usually involves a persistent feeling of anxiety or dread, which can interfere with daily life. It is not the same as occasionally worrying about things or experiencing anxiety due to stressful life events. People living with GAD experience frequent anxiety for months, if not years.

Symptoms of GAD include:
- Feeling restless, wound-up, or on-edge
- Being easily fatigued
- Having difficulty concentrating
- Being irritable
- Having headaches, muscle aches, stomach aches, or unexplained pains
- Difficulty controlling feelings of worry
- Having sleep problems, such as difficulty falling or staying asleep

Panic Disorder
People with Panic Disorder have frequent and unexpected panic attacks. Panic attacks are sudden periods of intense fear, discomfort, or sense of losing control even when there is no clear danger or trigger. Not everyone who experiences a panic attack will develop panic disorder.

During a panic attack, a person may experience:
- Pounding or racing heart
- Sweating
- Trembling or tingling
- Chest pain
- Feelings of impending doom

- Feelings of being out of control

People with Panic Disorder often worry about when the next attack will happen and actively try to prevent future attacks by avoiding places, situations, or behaviours they associate with panic attacks. Panic attacks can occur as frequently as several times a day or as rarely as a few times a year.

Social Anxiety Disorder
Social anxiety disorder is an intense, persistent fear of being watched and judged by others. For people with social anxiety disorder, the fear of social situations may feel so intense that it seems beyond their control. For some people, this fear may get in the way of going to work, attending school, or doing everyday things.

People with social anxiety disorder may experience:
- Blushing, sweating, or trembling
- Pounding or racing heart
- Stomach aches
- Rigid body posture or speaking with an overly soft voice
- Difficulty making eye contact or being around people they don't know
- Feelings of self-consciousness or fear that people will judge them negatively

Phobia-related disorders
A phobia is an intense fear of—or aversion to—specific objects or situations. Although it can be realistic to be anxious in some circumstances, the fear people with phobias feel is out of proportion to the actual danger caused by the situation or object.

People with a phobia:
- May have an irrational or excessive worry about encountering the feared object or situation

- Take active steps to avoid the feared object or situation

Experience immediate intense anxiety upon encountering the feared object or situation
- Endure unavoidable objects and situations with intense anxiety

There are several types of phobias and phobia-related disorders:

Specific phobias (sometimes called simple phobias):
As the name suggests, people who have a specific phobia have an intense fear of, or feel intense anxiety about, specific types of objects or situations. Some examples of specific phobias include the fear of:
- ·Flying
- ·Heights
- ·Specific animals, such as spiders, dogs, or snakes
- ·Receiving injections
- ·Blood.

Social Anxiety Disorder (previously called social phobia):
People with Social Anxiety Disorder have a general intense fear of, or anxiety toward, social or performance situations. They worry that actions or behaviours associated with their anxiety will be negatively evaluated by others, leading them to feel embarrassed. This worry often causes people with social anxiety to avoid social situations. Social anxiety disorder can manifest in a range of situations, such as within the workplace or the school environment.

Agoraphobia:
People with agoraphobia have an intense fear of two or more of the following situations:
- Using public transportation
- Being in open spaces
- Being in enclosed spaces
- Standing in line or being in a crowd

- Being outside of the home alone

People with agoraphobia often avoid these situations, in part, because they think being able to leave might be difficult or impossible in the event they have panic-like reactions or other embarrassing symptoms. In the most severe form of agoraphobia, an individual can become housebound.

Separation Anxiety Disorder:

Separation anxiety is often thought of as something that only children deal with. However, adults can also be diagnosed with Separation Anxiety Disorder. People with separation anxiety disorder fear being away from the people they are close to. They often worry that something bad might happen to their loved ones while they are not together. This fear makes them avoid being alone or away from their loved ones. They may have bad dreams about being separated or feel unwell when separation is about to happen.

Illness Anxiety Disorder:

Illness anxiety disorder, sometimes called hypochondriasis or health anxiety, is worrying excessively that you are or may become seriously ill. You may have no physical symptoms. Or you may believe that normal body sensations or minor symptoms are signs of severe illness, even though a thorough medical exam doesn't reveal a serious medical condition.

You may experience extreme anxiety that body sensations, such as muscle twitching or fatigue, are associated with a specific, serious illness. This excessive anxiety — rather than the physical symptom itself — results in severe distress that can disrupt your life.

Illness Anxiety Disorder is a long-term condition that can fluctuate in severity. It may increase with age or during times of stress.

Symptoms

Symptoms of illness anxiety disorder involve preoccupation with the idea that you're seriously ill, based on normal body sensations (such as a noisy stomach) or minor signs (such as a minor rash). Signs and symptoms may include:

- Being preoccupied with having or getting a serious disease or health condition
- Worrying that minor symptoms or body sensations mean you have a serious illness
- Being easily alarmed about your health status
- Finding little or no reassurance from doctor visits or negative test results
- Worrying excessively about a specific medical condition or your risk of developing a medical condition because it runs in your family
- Having so much distress about possible illnesses that it's hard for you to function
- Repeatedly checking your body for signs of illness or disease
- Frequently making medical appointments for reassurance — or avoiding medical care for fear of being diagnosed with a serious illness
- Avoiding people, places or activities for fear of health risks
- Constantly talking about your health and possible illnesses
- Frequently searching the internet for causes of symptoms or possible illnesses

Selective Mutism:

A somewhat rare disorder associated with anxiety is Selective Mutism. Selective mutism occurs when people fail to speak in specific social situations despite having normal language skills. Selective mutism usually occurs before the age of 5 and is often associated with extreme shyness, fear of social embarrassment, compulsive traits, withdrawal, clinging behaviour, and temper tantrums. People diagnosed with selective mutism are often also diagnosed with other anxiety disorders.

Transformative Healing with Bach essences can heal each of the above types.

Each type needs to be addressed with some specific essences, in addition to the ones mentioned above. For example, Red Chestnut for Separation Anxiety Disorder, Larch for Performance Anxiety Disorder and Heather for Illness Anxiety Disorder.

Write to **reachme@indroneil.com** describing your anxiety to get individualised composites that can heal you completely from the root.

ACKNOWLEDGEMENT

I acknowledge the contribution of my students, Aarti Kiri Saini, Dr. Ayesha Irshad and Mira Swaroop, during the intense research we carried out as a team, to get to the Bach Flower essences that can possibly heal the mental and physical causes for physical ailments.

www.ingramcontent.com/pod-product-compliance
Lightning Source LLC
LaVergne TN
LVHW071321080526
838199LV00079B/646